Reminiscences of Schleiermacher

by Dr. Friedrich Lücke

Translated by William Farrer

Copyright © 2018 Beloved Publishing
All rights reserved. No part of this book may be reproduced, scanned, or distributed in any printed or electronic form without permission.
Printed in the United States of America
Columbus, OH
ISBN: 978-1-63174-171-5

TABULAR SKETCH

OF THE

CHIEF FACTS AND DATES IN THE LIFE OF SCHLEIERMACHER.

1768. Nov. 21, FRIEDRICH DANIEL ERNST SCHLEIERMACHER born at Breslau, in Silesia.
    Went to the school of the United Brethren at Niesky, in Upper Lusatia; and subsequently to the Theological Seminary of the same community at Gnadau, in Saxony.

1787. Left the Moravian Communion. Studied at the University of Halle, under Nösselt, Knapp, Eberhard, and Wolf.
    Became Tutor in the family of Count Dohna-Schlobitten, of Finkenstein in Prussia.
    Removed to Berlin, to the Seminary for Masters of Classical Schools (in the capacity of Assistant-Teacher).

1794. His ordination. Assistant-Minister at Landsberg on the Warthe, in Brandenburg.

1796–1802. Preacher at the Charité (the principal Hospital) in Berlin. Assisted the elder Sack (afterwards Bishop Sack) in translating "Blair's Sermons." Issued a translation of Fawcett's "Sermons," (Berlin, 1798). Took part with the brothers Schlegel in the "Athenæum." Published his "Discourses on Religion," (Berlin, 1799); "Monologues," (Berlin, 1800); "Letters of a Preacher residing out of Berlin," (an *occasional* production—Berlin, 1800); and a first collection of "Sermons," (Berlin, 1801). He also agreed to join Friedrich Schlegel in translating Plato, but afterwards undertook the work alone.

1802. Court-Chaplain (Minister of the Court-Church) at Stolpe, in Pomerania.

1803. "First Lines of a Criticism of the Doctrine of Morals, as hitherto treated," (Berlin).

1804.	"Two Non-Prejudicative Opinions," &c., (Berlin). First volume of Plato. Declined a call to the University of Würzburg. Appointed University Preacher, and Professor Extraordinary of Theology and Philosophy at Halle.
1806.	"Christmas, a Dialogue," (Halle).
1807.	(Halle attached to the Kingdom of Westphalia). Returned to Berlin, and lectured there. "Critical Letter on the so-called First Epistle of Paul to Timothy," (Berlin, 1807). "Occasional Thoughts on Universities, in the German sense," (Berlin, 1808).
1809.	Minister of Trinity Church, Berlin. His marriage.
1810.	Professor in the New University of Berlin. Attached to the Ministry of the Interior for the Department of Public Instruction.
1811.	Member of the Academy of Sciences. "Brief Outline of the Study of Theology."
1814.	Secretary of the Philosophical Class in the Academy. Release from his connexion with the Ministry of the Interior.
1817.	"Critical Essay on the Gospel of Luke." President of the Berlin Synod.
1817–18.	Controversy with Von Ammon.
1821–22.	"Connected Exhibition of the Christian Faith, according to the Principles of the Evangelical Church."
1828.	Establishment of the "Studien und Kritiken"—a genuine product of his spirit, though not directed by him.
1834.	Feb. 12. Died at Berlin. His remains are interred in the cemetery of his parish, at some little distance from the city on its southern side. A simple monument, with a bust in white marble, of exquisite workmanship (by Rauch), has been erected over his grave.

REMINISCENCES

OF

SCHLEIERMACHER.

OFTEN, within the present lustrum, has it been our painful lot to behold some of the most distinguished men of our nation depart from amongst us; precisely those to whom, in different departments of the intellectual life, the present generation is indebted for its peculiar character and progress.

Barthold Niebuhr, the great explorer of history, opens this series of illustrious dead; at the commencement of a season of commotion, in which more general calamity might possibly occasion the particular loss of this great man to be felt less at the moment, though the sorrow to which the event gave rise could not be wholly suppressed. Goethe, Hegel, and others, have followed him. Now, Schleiermacher, too, is no longer among us. Thus are the great personalities, the stays, the luminaries of our age, one after another, taken away from us. This is a circumstance which happens in accordance with the everlasting order of nature. Still, it is not on that account any the less painful. He who loves the heights and the mountains, descends unwillingly into the level plain. And yet this alternation of mountain and plain, of heights and levels, is, in the spiritual world also, order and law. The history of humanity pursues its course between concentration and origination in distinguished individuals, and gradual diffusion and developement in the mass. Thus has it been ordained, even from the beginning, by Divine wisdom and love. No one ought to complain of this arrangement; least of all he who has been taught by the Gospel to discern even in death the law of life, and in the evanescent kingdom of nature the everlasting kingdom of Divine grace.

Schleiermacher, at a recent Festival of the Dead,* while instructing and consoling a Christian assembly with regard to the loss of distinguished men, by a reference to the arrangements of the Divine kingdom, uttered these memorable words: "This, too, is God's arrangement,—that there exists among the children of men a great, yea, often a very great difference, as well in relation to the intellectual gifts with which God has furnished them, as to the position which he has assigned them, and to those external conditions of efficiency by which one man seems to be favoured more than another. This difference exists, and we dare not deny it; so that when we look at human affairs in a general point of view, we cannot say that one human life is of the same value as another. And this Divine arrangement—where could it have been more clearly manifested,—what could have been a stronger expression of it, than the difference which obtained between the Redeemer and all other

* The Festival of the Dead (Todtenfest, Gedächtniss-Feier der Verstorbenen) is an annual holiday of the Lutheran Church, from which it has passed over into, or been retained by, the United Evangelical Church of Prussia. It is a simple *commemoration* of the departed, with a view to the edification of the living; and seems to have been instituted, in accordance with that *conservative* principle by which the Lutheran system is so extensively characterized, in place of the Romanist festival of All Souls.—TR.

children of men? That was the highest point to which this diversity amongst men was to rise: that in the midst of the sinful race of men the Word was to become flesh,—that the express image of God was to walk amongst them. In comparison with this difference, every other may well disappear; and yet he who was thus distinguished, was scarcely permitted to attain the bloom of manhood, but was then to be taken away hence again. And what did he send in his room? By what means was the work which he had begun, to be now further carried on? He sent the Spirit of Truth; he poured out upon his disciples this Spirit, who took of that which was his, and made it clear to them,—who distributed gifts, and, according to his good pleasure, left not himself without witness, in a greater or smaller degree, in one and another. And thus it is, too, in all human affairs. Oh! when we call up before our minds, as a whole and in detail, the chequered web of our social affairs, consisting as it does of manifold complications, truly, how much seems often to rest on *one* beloved head! How often is the experience repeated, that upon the determination of a single individual, upon the fact of its coming to maturity or the contrary, a large part of the immediately ensuing course of human affairs depends,—war and peace, order or destruction, prosperity or ruin! Thus does it happen with regard to the civic concerns of men. The case is the same, too, if we have regard to the cultivation of their mental powers; in which, also, it often happens that one man outshines all others by a great example, and levels paths which were before blocked up: but it is necessary that he should be protected in his activity for a certain time, if the newly-opened field is not to be buried again under rubbish, and nothing to remain but what existed before him. Let us not forget, however, that on the one hand the Redeemer was the culminating point, the highest summit of this Divine arrangement; but that he was also, on the other hand, the being through whom the prophecy was to receive its accomplishment,—that every valley should be filled up, and every height be made plain. And the more the community of man is developed,—the more widely the points of friendly contact, which as a common bond of union embrace all, extend,—the greater the influences which diffuse themselves from every part over the whole—so much the smaller does the influence of individual men become. Most of all is this intended to be the case, most of all is it actually the case, in the Church of the Lord, with regard to all that belongs to the concerns of salvation. It is true that even here, we see how, immediately in the room of the Saviour, the Spirit, poured out by him, moulded as its especial instruments only his apostles and some *few* individuals besides; and subsequently, too, we see that even the Church of Christ, from time to time, fell into such outward entanglements or such inward obscurations, that it became necessary for the Spirit of God to impart to individuals an especial energy, to kindle up an especially clear light in *one*, or in *a few* souls, in order that thus there might proceed from certain particular points a new life, which should continue to diffuse itself, should pervade the darkness, and, in the name of the Lord, awaken those who were dead to a new and fresh life again. But this is what constitutes our true confidence in the kingdom of God and its continuance,—that there are continually *fewer and fewer* of these disturbances, and that for this reason the necessity that individuals should be prominent in the kingdom of the Lord, also becomes more rare. If the

Spirit of God is continually to advance in the accomplishment of his work in the human race, his influence must be exercised upon men more and more on every hand [all-sidedly], his presence and operation must be capable of being perceived in every human life; and in the same measure must the disparity diminish amongst those who have found salvation in the name of the Lord, and are now seeking to diffuse that salvation more widely throughout the world. *Therefore, as often as we derive from the life and activity of any individual, the feeling that he is, in a greater or smaller degree, an especial instrument of God and of his Spirit, it is very possible that when the period of his activity comes to an end, a feeling of anxiety may arise in our hearts; but this anxiety is not the product of faith. Faith ought to know that the Lord, when he recalls one, also calls and appoints another; and he will never be at a loss for instruments to accomplish that which, in his Son and through him, is already accomplished everlastingly, and in the progress of time shall be ever more and more accomplished, through the increasingly equable co-operation of human energies, enlightened and directed by God.*"

Thus has the Christian sage, by his truly prophetic interpretation of the arrangements of the Divine kingdom, consoled us by anticipation, as it were, for our loss of him, and taken away from our remembrance and contemplation of him that sting, which, apart from the influence of Christian faith and hope, would have been all the more painful, in proportion to the greatness of the loss which we suffer through his death.

Schleiermacher belongs to that class of highly-gifted men who, in every direction in which their outward and inward calling leads them, diffuse light and life, create, arrange, and rule. His was one of the kingly, dominant natures. He was active in the most various departments and directions; he was distinguished and preeminent in them all. He was a learned theologian and a preacher of the word of God, a philosopher and philologer; he is known to the mass of the public as a talented writer upon the most important affairs of the day; and as a man of business, too, he was, in his own circle, beloved and highly esteemed.

It is not my purpose to set forth the great gifts and merits of Schleiermacher, completely and in every aspect. This is the business of an exact biography, for the production of which there will be no lack either of ability of or inclination, among those who constituted the more familiar circle of his latter years. I confine myself to that department in which Schleiermacher was, from the very first, at home; that to which, as to inward and outward vocation, he especially belonged: the department of Theology and the Church. In this department, he marks an *epoch* as few else have done. Dr. Neander, just after he had received intelligence of the death of his beloved instructor and colleague, accompanied the announcement of it to his hearers with these words: "The man is departed, from whom will be dated, for the future, a new epoch in theology." There will not be wanting those who, from ignorance, or petty jealousy, or party spirit, will deny this affirmation. But I anticipate, without anxiety, that the more his efficient activity shall unfold itself in its entire extent and connexion, posterity, with adequate knowledge, and without envy or partiality, will confirm the verdict pronounced in the first moment of sorrow. It will, it must declare him to be the man with whom a new tendency, in Theology and in the Church, had its energetic commencement.

In general, Schleiermacher marks the *transition* of German Protestant Theology from the more *negative-critical dispersing and destroying*, tendency to that *reconstructive, positive reformation* with which we are now occupied. This reformation includes two elements; a regression and a progress. By the regression involved, I mean the renewed reception of positive Christianity into the whole depth and capacity of the devout mind; the restoration of severe, connected Christian thinking, and the reanimation of the idea of ecclesiastical fellowship. These are the unalterable elements of every healthy Christian life. Our Protestant Theology and Church are built upon them. They can never become *lost* in the Church of the Lord. But they were, for a time, more or less obscured, scattered, and deprived of strength, among ourselves. The problem of the present is, to animate, to collect, to strengthen them anew. This, however, is not possible, apart from the living progress of that science, which, advancingly with the progress of time, separates all that is purely human, all that is accidental and inessential, all that is imposed and arbitrary from the original Word of God, and, amidst the letter and the form, makes the living spirit free and active; but which, at the same time, just by means of the spirit thus made free, preserves and animates the original form, and while opening up the understanding of the Word of God in its height and depth, on the other hand closes the path of contradiction and doubt for ever. The mode of procedure of this science will be chiefly critical. *All* criticism is not advancing and reformatory. We have become acquainted with a criticism which, being destitute of Christian spirit or contents, thought to understand and judge the fulness of the Gospel by means of emptiness, faith by unbelief, truth by imaginations and sudden fancies. In this process there was nothing salutary, but, on the contrary, retrogression and corruption. The most painful experiences have convinced us, that the *true* criticism proceeds only from the fulness and concentration of Christian life and thought; that only by diving, humbly and believingly, to the depths of the Divine Word, does Christian science acquire the *strength* and the *right* to understand the truth of the Gospel, and in accordance with this truth to judge and condemn all error, and everything that is unchristian in its character.

Schleiermacher's youth falls within the period in which the criticism that was first set in motion by Semler with regard to Christian history, and by Kant with regard to philosophy, commenced its salutary conflict with the earlier orthodoxy, which had now become soulless and insipid. It was the same period in which, after long repose, all the elements of civil, literary, and ecclesiastical life were vehemently shaken as by a thunder-storm, and the old forms, ordinances, and customs went to pieces in our father-land too. Schleiermacher, although educated in a community which, from its entire character, was most of all removed from these revolutionary agitations, and closed against them, could not withdraw himself from a participation in them; the less so, since he belonged by nature to those independent and impelling spirits who produce agitation even if they find none, and whose vital element is that of free inquiry, investigation, and dubitation. In the Dedication of his "Discourses on Religion" to the friend of his youth, Gustav Brinkmann of Stockholm, who was educated along with himself amongst the United Brethren, he reminds the latter of that season "in which the mode of thinking of both young men was developed in a mutual fellowship, and in which, having broken away by the force of personal courage from a like yoke, and frankly seeking the truth, unbribed by any regard to mere authority, they began to call forth within themselves that harmony with the universe which their inward feeling prophetically placed before them as their appropriate aim, and which life ought to express ever more and more perfectly in every direction." But amidst all the impulsive energy of his liberty-loving, critical genius, which even in the midst of that confined and quiet community drew him into the agitations of the time, and which afterwards, when he had returned to the great fellowship of the Protestant Church and the University, constrained him to a lively and thorough participation in all the excited movements of the age, especially in all its scientific investigations, inquiries, and doubtings,—he yet continued to be inwardly and inseparably bound to the equally mighty energy of that devout disposition with which God had endowed him, and to which the community already referred to had itself given the first powerful excitement, as well as its definite direction towards that which is the everlasting *contents* [q.d. sum and substance] of life, and which is found in the Saviour, and in fellowship with him. I have never been able to read without heartfelt emotion, what Schleiermacher says in his "Discourses on Religion," in grateful remembrance of the religious education which he had received amongst the United Brethren. "Piety," he says, "was the maternal womb in whose sacred obscurity my young life was nourished, and prepared for the world which was as yet closed to it; in this element my spirit breathed, before it had as yet found its particular department in science and in the experience of life; this was my aid, when I began to sift the faith of my ancestors, and to purify my thoughts and feelings from the rubbish of former ages; this remained to me, when even the God and the immortality of my childhood disappeared from before the doubting eye;* it led me undesignedly into active life; it showed me how I ought to hold myself sacred, with my talents and defects, in my undivided existence, and through it alone have I learned friendship and love."

Thus were Schleiermacher's nature and life impelled and governed by two equally powerful forces. In the case of an intellect so thoroughly healthy, there could be no talk of sacrificing the one to the other; but only of maintaining, protecting, and perfecting each, within its rightful province. Schleiermacher apprehended very early the great problem of uniting, without confusion, without mutual injury or hindrance, free scientific investigation with that piety which is governed by the Word of God and of Christ, in such a manner, that the contradiction and the hostility in which they had become involved by the movements of the age should increasingly disappear. The solution of this problem was, most strictly, the work of his whole life. He sought it in the difficult way of *separation*, pursuing both elements in their *particularity*, as far as to their highest and deepest points of *unity*. He separated theology and philosophy, faith and speculation, Church and State, with all that dialectical acuteness with which he was gifted; but, while he assigned to each of the two contrasted objects its peculiar sphere, in which, undisturbed by the other, it was, of itself, to unfold and to perfect itself, he held fast, with equal clearness and cordiality, the great assumption of the believing soul,—that as in the innermost

---

* Any one who, being without any personal experience in such matters, might possibly misunderstand this passage, stands corrected by the observation relating to it, in the explanatory Notes [appended by Schleiermacher to the third edition of the work here referred to].

root of the spirit's life the two are one, so also must perfect unity and reconciliation spring as a necessary result from every healthy developement of the diverse. But, seeing that he regarded this unity and reconciliation neither as consisting in a speculative formula of faith with which all thinking should *commence*, nor as an easy spoil of which any indolent or frivolous person may make himself master by means of *half*-efforts,—but rather as the infinite problem and the last result of a critical *labour in common* on the part of *all*, in every department of life, —it might easily happen that, because he was occupied chiefly in the labour of separating and sundering as *his* immediate work, the unobservant should think themselves obliged to reckon him amongst the disuniting, disturbing, and disrupting, rather than as belonging to the truly reconciling, constructive, and reforming spirits of the age. Any one, however, that considered his mode of thinking and his activity in their comprehensiveness and totality, must soon become aware that he was one of those great men in whose peculiar character is concentrated whatever is noblest and best in their age, and whose particular life-problem is at the same time the common, highest problem of the age; that is, in the present instance, the problem of *reformation*, by means of an equally energetic *separation* and *reconciliation* of certain things which form an antithesis with each other. His merit consists precisely in this,—that he not merely apprehended with perfect clearness the reformational necessities and the reformational elements of the age in the department of Christianity, but also, in a distinguished manner, by his peculiar theological thinking and working, satisfied the one and gave form to the other. In any other vocation than that of the theologian, Schleiermacher would still have become great and preeminent. The age in which he made choice of his particular calling, was the same in which Spalding found it necessary to convince people as to the *utility* of the office of the preacher. The State held out to his view more brilliant paths than the Church; and any other science might easily have appeared to his mind of greater promise than theology, in which, at that time more than at any other, want of refinement, tedious controversy, and a destructive tendency, had the upper hand. But he made choice of the theological, ecclesiastical vocation, because his inmost nature impelled him to it. Theology and the Church were from an early period of life the innermost centre of his activity; his love towards them grew with his years; philosophical and philological studies were with him no mere collateral or amateur occupation, but still his special proficiency in these respects merely served to adorn and to complete his theological and ecclesiastical mastery.

Schleiermacher did not accomplish the reformation of the age, in Theology and in the Church, *alone*. No great man stands alone, without help and fellowship in his age. But Schleiermacher, with true originality, went on in advance; he, by way of eminence, stimulated and directed the process of theological and ecclesiastical re-edification, and first moulded for himself those who were the most distinguished helpers and companions of his work. He founded a school, inasmuch as, especially from his first appearance as a teacher of theology and preacher at Halle, he assembled around him and attached to him, by means of his discourses and writings, a multitude of enthusiastic hearers and admirers, who, roused and animated by him, have wrought and are yet working in his spirit. Probably there are few among those who have become serviceable or auxiliary to the new movement in

Theology and the Church, who do not owe their chief stimulus to the lectures or the writings of Schleiermacher. Indeed, mediately, all the more recent theologians have become his pupils, not excepting those who now follow another and even an opposite tendency. The stimulus put forth by him is at least consciously or unconsciously *implied*, in the case of all. If he has founded a school in *this* sense, he has *not* done so in any *other*. It was his manner, to work rather by stimulating than by prescribing, rather in the way of diffusion and emancipation, than in that of contraction, exclusion, and restraint. He never wished to found that kind of school which, with conscious purpose, makes its appearance as a *party*, secludes itself within a certain fixed *method*,* and *excludes* every modifying influence from without. For this,—notwithstanding all the strength and keenness of his subjectivity,—his regard for the Church and for science was too high, his intellect too free and too comprehensive. Even as, amidst all the certainty and fulness of that which he had *found*, he was and continued to the last to be himself a *seeker* ($\zeta\eta\tau\eta\tau\iota\varkappa\acute{o}\varsigma$),—even as he counted free individuality amongst the noblest of life's blessings,—so, in his labours, his chief object was simply this, to form every one to be a seeker after truth in earnestness and love,—to make the individuality of each so free and vigorous, that he should be able, amidst every excitement from without, freely to possess the truth after his own fashion. Free, independent disciples were what he sought to attract; slavish repeaters and imitators inspired him with disgust. But there are not a few amongst his disciples who, although they were at first stirred up by his agency in favour of the new

* *Mannerism* would hardly have been too strong a rendering of the word here employed.—Tr.

movement, have subsequently, to a certain extent, fallen into contradiction and conflict with him. This circumstance has occasioned sorrow to many a friend of Schleiermacher; most of all in those cases in which it was observable with regard to his opponents, that they had either stolen their best weapons from him, or learnt from him how to use them. In *his* spirit, we can find fault with them only when, ungrateful for what they have received, they have set aside the fellowship of *love* with him. With regard to diversity of *tendencies*, and deviations from his *opinions*, no one was of a better courage than Schleiermacher himself.* He was not without sensibility as it respected affectionate recognition and attachment; misunderstanding and unkind separation had power to cause him pain; but he felt a sincere rejoicing in the existence of a multiplicity of relations and tendencies, of oppositions and honourable conflicts. Apart from that which was furnished by the *momentum* of intellectual liberty in general, there was in himself an altogether special natural reason for this phenomenon,

---

* "It seems to me,"—he says in the Notes to his "Discourses on Religion," p. 345,—" especially in every time of a greater excitement of the religious life, such as has undeniably commenced among us now,—to be in the highest degree necessary for the personal comfort of all those who exercise a perceptible religious influence, whether it be officially, or without any external, and only by virtue of their inward calling, that they should elevate themselves to this more liberal mode of thinking," (see the beautiful passage concerning mastery and discipleship within the domain of religion, in the Discourses, p. 112), " in order that they may not be surprised, if many of those whose first stimulus has been received from them, nevertheless afterwards find it necessary to take up a considerably different mode of thinking and feeling ere they can arrive at full satisfaction. *Let every one rejoice in that he has excited life*, for by this he approves himself to be an instrument of the Divine Spirit; but let none suppose that it lies within his power to determine the *form* which this life shall assume."

and I am persuaded that Schleiermacher was acquainted with it. He had, in a peculiar manner, united in himself the various elements of theology, and bound them up into a noble whole. But that which in him, by nature and by industry, was intimately bound up together, was not so in all. Along with the great men who, by reason of their nature and character, stand in the *centre* of things, there exists always upon the circumference and within the circle the multitude of those who, although they are attracted and determined by the centre, ever pursue that one side and tendency only which is most in harmony with themselves, or of which they first became masters, and in doing so, lose all the rest, and, in the end, the centre by which the connexion is formed. Thus it happened with regard to Schleiermacher. Many whom he had, in the first instance, won back in favour of positive Christianity, or to whom he had opened up the profound source of the religious life in the immediate feeling, or to whom he had rendered clear and dear the vigorous connexion, and truth in the Spirit, of the Church's system of doctrine, found themselves so powerfully excited and impelled thereby, that in following out this tendency they overlooked and lost the other (the critical) side of the system,—which he, from the central position in which he had his life, held fast with an equal degree of attachment and energy; nay, in the end, estranged, they came to regard the latter as something hostile. It is a circumstance worthy of remark, and one which furnishes a testimony in favour of the Christian *vitality* of his mode of teaching, that amongst those who attached themselves especially to the *critical* side of his theology, and made a further advance in *that* direction, there was probably not one who did not at the same time hold fast and cherish the *religious* and positive ecclesiastical *momentum* which the system contains. But as Schleiermacher, from that living centre in which he had his position, readily perceived the one-sided tendencies of the age, and, when they threatened to obtain the preponderance, held it his duty to combat them, if not immediately, yet mediately, by bringing out with greater force the opposite side of the question,—it might easily come to pass that any one who saw him contending, with decision and zeal, in the direction referred to, might suppose, (especially when the observer was himself attacked by the wrathful Ajax) that he was involved in contradiction and hostility towards the truth which he had himself on other occasions defended. Thus have misunderstandings, silent and uttered enmities and separations, arisen in the midst of those who were in other respects akin to him. On this subject, he himself, in his own way, observes:—" If a one-sided tendency becomes too strongly prominent, it is my—I know not whether I ought to say *manner* or *un*-manner,* from a natural fear lest the ship in which we are all sailing should capsize, to go over to the other side with as much force as is possible with my small weight." Even these harmless words of moderating and preserving truth and love have been misunderstood, and cried down as an expression—coming to light at last—of his inward wavering and vacillation; by those who see in the diverse tendencies of the age nothing but corruption, and in the antagonist position against which they are furiously contending, nothing but untruth and apostasy from Christianity. Schleiermacher was far removed from the

* A literal rendering (for which I must intreat the reader's kind indulgence) of the play upon words contained in the original. *Unart* signifies properly "bad habit," or "naughty trick;" a meaning which our legitimate English word "unmannerly" will probably suggest in connection with the term employed above.—Tr.

indulgence of this haughty manner. Great as was the weight he brought to the side on which he directly contended, still he never forgot the centre of the true reformative theology, of that which unites all the elements of Christian life and thought; but, often as he marched forth to conflict in different directions, he always retreated again to this as his proper standpoint, and never forsook the fountain of the living Gospel. He had but two foes against which, as such, he continually renewed the conflict, even to the last man; the *servitude of the letter*, which denies the *liberty* of the Gospel, and the *frivolous superficiality* which denies its *everlasting truth*.

Proceeding now to consider in detail the scientific, theological, and the practical, ecclesiastical activity of Schleiermacher,—and first of all to characterize the former as it presents itself in his writings,—we find its characteristic starting-point in his "Discourses on Religion, addressed to the cultivated class of its Despisers,"[*]—a work which has become famous alike through praise and through censure. It appeared for the first time in 1799, then in 1806, and again in 1821; the third time with illustrative and vindicatory annotations. The work, to a certain extent, quite belongs to the period in which it had its origin; it bears the stamp of the relationships and of the society in the midst of which it was first written. The period was precisely that in which it was still regarded, by a circle far from small, as a greater mark of intellect and refinement to *oppose* religion, especially positive Christianity,—or, at the best, to commend it to the authorities as a means of discipline to be applied to the vulgar,—than to defend it as the necessary foundation and stay of all true culture for humanity. The prevailing schools of theology, whether

[*] Reden über die Religion, an die Gebildeten unter ihren Verächtern.

orthodox or heterodox, were little suited to dissipate the frivolous prejudices of the age against religion. Ecclesiastical orthodoxy maintained a firm hold upon notions and formulas which, by reason of the real progress of the age, had actually lost their power and vitality in the Church. Heterodoxy,* on the other hand,—in its philosophical, as in its historico-critical form,—was at that time preponderantly occupied in the work of pulling down; it wanted the living idea of religion, the divination, the enthusiasm, which would have enabled it to build up something new and something better; nay, it was to a certain extent occupied with the project of despoiling religion of its principality,—of banishing it from the *centre* of *life*, into the side and back-buildings of *science*, or of a self-existing *morality*. This suffices to determine, in general, the purpose, contents, and tone of the Discourses. Schleiermacher felt himself constrained to take the field with the two-fold warrior-might of a fresh, youthful enthusiasm in the cause of religion, and a keen, lively dialectic, to discover and to conquer anew, as it were, the domain of religion for the educated classes, to present religion to view in its true, original seat, freed from the misunderstandings and disfigurements perpetrated by foes and friends, and to inflame such as were in any way susceptible, with new love for the object thus presented. It seemed as if this would not have been possible to him, without the possession of an uncommonly brilliant eloquence. This quality, at least, has been admired even by his oppo-

* It may be proper to remind the reader, that Schleiermacher (and presumably also his friend and disciple) employs the terms *orthodoxy* and *heterodoxy* in a sense different from that invidious one which is commonly attached to them. With him they correspond in the main to the *conservative*, and the *reformatory*, element or tendency, respectively. See Brief Outline, §§ 203—206.—Tr.

nents, and probably contributed essentially to excite an interest in the subject, even in minds of the more inaccessible class. Friedrich Schlegel said at the time, "They are discourses, the first of their kind that we have in German; full of energy and fire, and yet very artistic, in a style which would not be unworthy of one of the ancients."—The society in which Schleiermacher then lived, was formed by the companionship of those enterprising and perhaps somewhat presumptuous spirits, who published and enforced their decided antagonism to the mental poverty and Philistinism* of the age, by a bold and fearless course of polemics in the "Athenæum." This explains to a certain extent that polemical form, that boldness and daringness of assertion, which made the Discourses as much a scandal to the so-called sober and prudent people, as they were a delight to minds of a more youthful order. But whether repelling or attracting, they were for all in the highest degree stimulating. Undeniably, the manner in which Schleiermacher apprehended and represented the nature of religion in these discourses, was a product of his own personal developement up to that time, and a faithful image of his own individuality. Friedrich Schlegel called it, in this respect, "the most *characteristic* book we have—a book of an infinite subjectivity." A man who had attained to the consciousness of possessing religion within himself, in the profoundest

---

* Most readers, probably, are aware that the *Philister* (Philistines) are the "Town" of the German seats of learning, in opposition to the Professors and *Burschen*, or Students,—to whom we might apply the familiar epithet "Gown," if they were but provided with the graceful and scholar-like costume to which it refers. *Philistinism* (Philisterei) accordingly, is tantamount to a want of learning, of intellectual expansion and activity, of high enthusiasm; it is the *Materialistic* tendency in its broadest compass and manifestation.—TR.

depth of his soul, as the supremely sacred domestic *hearth* of his life,—*anterior* to all the speculation of science, and anterior to all action, as being itself the deeper source of both,—such a man *could* not think of it as a *product* or as an *auxiliary supplement* of knowledge and action. He assigned to it, as independent sovereign over the entire life, the feeling as its original, essential seat; feeling, however, regarded [not according to the popular use of the term, but] as constituting the central and kindling point, the inmost root of the soul. In order that he might be able to bring to recognition as such everything that exists amongst men under the character of religion, and, in the spirit of love, to take up into the *idea* of religion even its lowest gradations, he apprehended this idea, subjectively as broadly, and objectively as generally, as it was at all possible for him to do. But since he was himself conscious of possessing religion, in its definiteness and truth, only as a Christian and within the Christian church, it was necessary that he should endeavour to show that religion, universally, has an *actual* and *vital* existence only through the medium of *positive* religion and of *fellowship*. In the Discourses, the influence exerted by his studies of Plato, Spinoza, Kant, Jacobi, and Fichte, shows itself unmistakeably. These authors, however, merely *aided* him, in the way of stimulus and of culture, to attain to a proper consciousness of his *own* distinctive peculiarity. Whoever reads the Discourses attentively and without prejudice, will easily perceive that in his mode of thinking with regard to religion, Schleiermacher is neither Jacobian nor Fichtean, neither Platonist nor Spinozist, but completely *himself;* and moreover himself with that soul of his deeply rooted in Christianity. It is precisely on account of these Discourses most of all, that he has been charged with Pantheism; often without reflection, but sometimes deliberately and in earnest. Certainly, here and there, appearances, and even particular expressions, are against him. But it is only the man who leaves out of account the particular stand-point and design of the Discourses in the age in which they first appeared, and mistakenly regards certain of their extreme boundary-points as constituting their centre and substance,—the man who declares *every* more profound and intimate apprehension of the (in the religious soul indissoluble) relation between God and the universe to be Pantheism, and is better pleased with any cold, mechanical theory of the universe which dispenses with the living presence and operation of God therein, than with anything which has the effect of softening down and limiting rigid and one-sided notions,—it is only such a man that can regard Pantheism as expressing the true and permanent character of Schleiermacher's sentiments. At all events, after the explanations which Schleiermacher has given in reference to this matter in the third edition of the work, it is impossible for any one to repeat the accusation, without manifesting stubbornness and violating charity. The Discourses belong, by all means, to one of the *earlier* stages of developement and of progress in the life of Schleiermacher; and it is by a reference to this fact that they must be explained. After the composition of his Dogmatics it would no longer have been possible for him to write them,—nor, indeed, would it have been necessary. They are apologies rather for religion in general than for Christianity in particular, delivered, as it were, in the fore-court of theology,—I might almost say in the fore-court of the Heathen; but still they contain already, distinctly enough, the peculiar bases and essential tendencies of his entire theology; and this explains the fact that when, in the year 1821, Schleiermacher,—who regarded the work as no longer needed by the age, in consequence of the changes which had taken place since it was written,—was notwithstanding obliged to take it in hand for the purpose of preparing a new edition, and came to compare this youthful labour with his *maturer* Christian thinking, he found in it, certainly, much to explain, much to modify and to excuse, in the notes which he then added, but still, essentially, nothing to repent of and nothing to surrender.

Up to the year 1804, he was perhaps known in the proper character of a learned theologian, only within certain limited circles. But from the time of his appearing, in that year, as a public teacher of theology at Halle, he awakened by his lectures, first the attention, and then the most devoted enthusiasm of the susceptible class of young men. I recollect very well how, at that season, some of my elder fellow-students, returning from Halle, spoke with enthusiastic praises of the new light that had arisen for them in the person of Schleiermacher. It was a circumstance involved in the history of his developement and his individuality, that, in addition to Systematic and Practical Theology, the Exegesis and Criticism of the New Testament received an especial share of his attention. His studies in this department were profound and comprehensive; but unquestionably they were directed rather towards the Greek and Christian, than towards the Hebrew and Old Testament side of the matter. He was no stranger to what is called scholarship in the stricter sense of the word; but, as he once playfully observed in writing to me, it was of no use to look for *Notices** from him. He read carefully such works as were connected in any way with his own department; but upon the principle of selection rather than of collection. And as he had, after the likeness of Plato, a soul which turned towards the Idea, and which possessed at the same time an artistic tendency,—everywhere searching after the living Idea, the connexion of the whole,—but seeking for this Idea, when found, the most appropriate, the most living, the purest Form,—so, even from the beginning, his mode of delineation, in the department of learned theology, was prevailingly artistic, graceful, and free from the constraint and the distraction of mind attendant upon the employment of learned citations. His " Critical Letter concerning the so-called First Epistle of Paul to Timothy," (1807) is composed in the style just described. It was by this specimen of his theological scholarship that he first made himself known to the learned world of theology; including even that portion of it which had not bestowed any particular attention upon his " Discourses on Religion." The specimen, however, was the specimen of a master. From the time of Semler onwards, the historical criticism of the Canon had been carried on with a large amount of freedom. Moreover, the critical difficulties presented by the Epistle in question, especially with regard to its historical relations, had been already noted, and Schmidt of Giessen had not been afraid at least to *doubt* its genuineness. But still the " Letter" was something new and unique in its way. It may be regarded as the first transplanting of that ingenious† criticism which

---

* *E. g.* such as might be expected from a learned and exact *bibliographer* or *antiquarian.*—Tr.

† In the higher sense of the word; bespeaking *genius.*—Tr.

had been employed by such masters as Bentley in the region of classical literature, to the literature of the New Testament. Up to this time, it had been the custom amongst theologians to subject to a sceptical criticism those Scriptures only which, in the ancient Church, had been regarded more or less as Antilegomena. But where, as in the case of the First Epistle to Timothy, the ancient Church gave testimony so unanimously that the book was genuine,—in such a case, even Semler's school did not venture to doubt. In order to remove the historical and exegetical difficulties presented by the Epistle, men chose rather to take refuge in hypotheses, than in suspicion. Schleiermacher, however, ventured upon a thorough-going, divinatory species of criticism. In this he disdained even the help which the absence of the Pastoral Epistles from the Canon of Marcion might have afforded him. As the suspicion had arisen in his mind in consequence of a connected study of the Pauline Epistles, and of the profoundly penetrating sympathy which he had sought to acquire with the whole character and manner of Paul, so, too, his argument against the genuineness of the Epistle was drawn from internal reasons for doubt; from the un-Pauline character of its thought and style, its want of connexion, the incongruity and indistinctness of its historical relations, and its suspicious resemblance (as of a compilation) to the other two Pastoral Epistles, &c. The criticism is so ingenious, the mode of presentation so lively and clear, so overpowering, that any one who gives himself up with but a certain measure of carelessness to the first impression, almost involuntarily agrees with the author. It is true that when we recollect ourselves, and examine the details more strictly, we perceive the weakness of particular points of the argument, the venturesomeness of certain particular assertions; we become suspicious of a criticism which deals with the Pauline Epistles as with classical writings, which assumes the existence of a finished and to us perfectly knowable *type* of the Pauline mode of speaking and of epistolizing, and—notwithstanding that our information is so defective—of a perfectly known and complete *circle* of historical relations as applying to the Apostle: but although the younger Planck and others have succeeded in bringing up a good deal in opposition to Schleiermacher's criticism, in defence of the Epistle, and towards the satisfying of men's minds respecting it, still, they have *not* succeeded in clearing away every disquieting suggestion, and the faith of the Church in the genuineness of the Epistle referred to has received a wound which, in spite of all the curative arts that have been applied hitherto, is not yet completely healed. But notwithstanding all the boldness of Schleiermacher's criticism, there was a *measure* in it. When, subsequently, Eichhorn rejected all three of the Pastoral Epistles as spurious, I recollect Schleiermacher told me that this appeared to him to be a going beyond all bounds, and that, in his opinion, any one who rejected the other two Pastoral Epistles gave up, by that act, the justifying reason and the basis for the criticism of the first of them. But whatever we may think as to the justifiableness and the result of Schleiermacher's critique,—a more ingenious, a more distinguished product of New Testament criticism (even so far as the *form* is concerned) we have not to show, anywhere. I have heard classical philologers speak of it as something of which they envied us the possession. The divinatory species of criticism, which this Letter has been the chief means of putting in motion among us, has its dangers, and least of all is it an occupation to be pursued by everybody. But it is necessary to the completeness of the theological Science of the Canon; and since there is no rational ground for regarding it as less necessary within the domain of theology than in that of classical literature, it must be imputed to Schleiermacher, as a real merit, that he introduced it among us in the manner in which he did. The historical criticism of the Christian Canon continued to form one of Schleiermacher's favourite occupations. Many a critical hint, many a critical inquiry and reply, of a like nature with his essay "On the Testimonies of Papias respecting our first two Gospels,"* may possibly yet lie hidden amongst his exegetical Lectures. As an author, he made a further application of this criticism to the Gospel of Luke, in relation to the difficult problem concerning the manner in which the synoptical Gospels had their origin; in his "Critical Essay on the Writings of Luke" (Part i. 1817). It is well known, how, especially from the time of Lessing downwards, this problem had been almost exhausted by a series of hypotheses; not solved, however, but only rendered more enigmatical. Schleiermacher, concurrently with Dr. Gieseler,† led back the investigation out of those airy regions into which men had been misled by Eichhorn's hypothesis of a single original Gospel, to the sure ground of history and exegesis. His hypothesis—as simple, as it is historically probable—is this: that our Gospels are to be regarded as *collections*, formed independently of one another, of smaller and larger

---

* In the Studien und Kritiken for 1832, Pt. 4. p. 735 *et seq.*

† Dr. Gieseler's "Historisch-kritischer Versuch über die Entstehung und die Frühern Schicksale der schriftlichen Evangelien" was published at Leipzig in 1818, its author being at that time Director of the Gymnasium at Cleve. The substantial agreement of his theory with that of Schleiermacher is sufficiently intimated in the text.—Tr.

evangelical *memorabilia* previously existing. He endeavoured to establish this hypothesis by applying it in the first instance to the Gospel of Luke. By going more deeply into the structure of this Gospel, and by comparing it with the other two, he attempted, in the most ingenious way, to discover in their original form and character the evangelical Memoirs which he supposed to form its basis; and to determine Luke's manner of proceeding in the collocation and arrangement of them. The *apologetical* interests of the sacred Scriptures have but *gained* by this attempt of his; not merely because, as a general principle, they never can do otherwise than gain by the spread of truth, but also because our conviction as to the goodness of Luke's sources of information, and as to the conscientiousness with which he employed them, has been essentially promoted by Schleiermacher's essay. It has been objected against this work, that its suggestions are often more ingenious than probable, especially with regard to the sections and junctions [of the Gospel], and to the original form of its sources. But it was partly in Schleiermacher's manner, and partly in the nature of such a first experiment, that the theory should be carried out in all strictness, even to the extreme. It is one advantage of these acute investigations, that they enable us to discern clearly *how far* we *may* go. This is always an important gain. Continued criticism, especially the uniform carrying out of Schleiermacher's method in the case of the other two Gospels, will infallibly lead to many modifications, limitations, corrections [of the views entertained by him]. But it is only by proceeding in the manner which he adopted, connecting the comparative study of the Gospels with an investigation as to the individual manner of each Evangelist in particular, that the critical problem presented by the Gospels will, with the progress of time, be determined more and more to the satisfaction of science and of the Church. But even if it should hereafter be found necessary to strike out other paths, —provided they be but paths of truth, the distinguished merit of Schleiermacher in his essential furtherance of this inquiry must always meet with grateful recognition.*

In consequence of a natural combination of criticism with exegesis, these treatises on the First Epistle to Timothy and on the Gospel of Luke, also contain specimens of Schleiermacher's exegetical method; occurring rather, however, merely *by the way*. Any one who has had the good fortune to hear his courses of exegetical lectures, will be able to give a better account of his exegetical method than I can. My knowledge of it (apart from the occasional specimens just referred to) is derived merely from the perusal of his essay on Col. i. 15—20,† and from the statements of those who have attended his lectures. The idea which I have formed of it to myself is the following. Schleiermacher knew of no other mode of expounding the Sacred Scriptures, than that in which there is a mutual interpenetration between a philological spirit and philological skill, on the one hand, and a living interest in the Canon as embodying the original, normal representation of Christianity, on the other. He declared expressly, in his encyclopædian course,‡ that exegesis, unaccompanied by a true interest on behalf of

---

* The English translator of the above work [reported to be the present Bishop of St David's, Dr C. Thirlwall] says in his Introduction, very truly, "It deserves to be studied as a specimen of exegetical criticism which has seldom been equalled, and which cannot fail to excite the admiration even of those who do not admit all its conclusions."

† See the Studien und Kritiken for 1832, p. 497 *et seq.*

‡ See his "Brief Outline," §§ 147, 148.—Tr.

theology and of Christianity, is just as idle and inadmissible, as it is when unconnected with a philological spirit and with philological skill. In his view, the thing to be aimed at in all interpretation consisted in this,— to apprehend correctly every individual thought along with its relation to the idea of the whole, and thus to *construct* for ourselves, in the way of imitation, the original act of composition. But though his attention was directed above all things to the solution of this chief problem in a really philological manner, he made it little or no part of the business of his exegetical lectures specially to investigate the *grammatical* and *historical elements* of this solution, but more or less taking these for granted, in order to avoid all diversion of attention, or touching upon them only in so far as they were of essential service to the hermeneutical operation, he went directly, in every case, to the construction* and delineation of the *thoughts* and their connexion. He carried out this process of construction with a preponderating regard to the *form* of the thoughts before him. The *ascetic, apologetical,* and *systematic developement* of these thoughts, he left for discourses better adapted to the purpose. In this respect, his *sermons* rendered essential service in the way of *completing* his exposition towards the more *real* [*material* as opposed to formal] and popular side of the subject. They are a treasure as it respects the exegetical developement of thought.—His scientific exposition was chiefly marked by a dialectic character, and rested on the assumption of certain

---

* Here, and in the context, this term is used to signify the process by which we *re*-construct, as it were, in our own minds, with as much accuracy as possible, a thought, or a system of thoughts, expressed or recorded by another. The many readers who do *not* need this comment will perhaps pardon its insertion, for the sake of the few who *do*.—Tr.

strict laws of thought and of composition, as applying to his author also. In this department of exposition he attained to distinguished excellence, and was indeed a *master*.—The hermeneutical operation consists of two equally essential movements of the mind,—which seem to exclude each other, but which in reality are inseparable; the *immergent* and the *emergent*, as I am disposed to call them. By the former I understand the entering fully, the sinking of one's self, as it were, into the spirit and the peculiar manner of the author. In order to this, a certain degree of self-renunciation, of self-surrender, is required; such as is to be found in the case of friendship. This is the first, the essential condition of all true understanding; which is all the purer and more objective in its character, the more the expositor, in the act referred to, denies himself and his own individuality and age. This hermeneutical self-denial, however, is not required to be (any more than that self-denial which is in the strictest sense moral) a *giving up* of one's proper self; but only an *expansion* of the latter. If this entering into the [position and spirit of the] author is not at the same time a *voluntary apprehension*, a true taking up into our proper self of that which was foreign to us, a personal, individual *appropriation*, it is fruitless, because it is more or less unconscious or unintelligent. The process of *exposition* is completed only by an individual *appropriation* [of the author's meaning]; the translation, as it were, of that which was foreign, into that which is our own. The highest perfection to which the process of exposition can attain, is, to apprehend the meaning of the author with full *objectivity*, (by a process of penetration, immergence), and to give it forth again with a like degree of *individuality* (emergence and appropriation). So long as there is no true, pure friendship, no complete establishment of identity, between the author and the expositor, the exposition is more or less in danger from the influences of misapprehension and nonapprehension. No one individual succeeds in the perfect solution of the exegetical problem in this its height and depth. In every expositor, even in him who gives himself up most completely to the influence of the author, there always remains behind an unconquered, uncompensated portion of his own individuality, by which the pure objectivity of the apprehension is interfered with. On the other hand, he who merely goes through the process of self-surrender, without any accompanying, vigorous appropriation, will be more or less deficient in the power of expounding what he has received, and thus bringing about an understanding of it on the part of others. The gifts which exposition requires are not distributed in an equal proportion. Schleiermacher belongs to the class of those who are far more strongly inclined towards a distinctive individuality of apprehension, than to self-surrender; who rather draw over the author to their own position, than allow themselves to be drawn by him. This method, provided it does not wholly neglect the endeavour to enter into the individuality of the author, has both its reasons and its advantages. It is precisely this circumstance,—the complete traversing of the contents of the New Testament Scriptures by a large number of competent *individual* and *original* apprehensions,—which leads to a growing understanding and appropriation of these contents within the Church. In so far, we must admit that Schleiermacher, by reason of the peculiarity and originality of his manner of apprehension, rendered important service to the cause of exegesis also. But this energetic individuality of his, which impressed itself upon every thing that came within his sphere, had precisely the effect of preventing him from entering into the views of the New Testament writers with that self-surrender, that self-forgetfulness, which is necessary in order that the expositor may give again in its purity, and free from all damage, the unfamiliar meaning, and the unfamiliar form. Amongst the writers of the New Testament, there was none that approached more nearly in character to himself than Paul; of the whole number, he most loved him. For that very reason, he has probably contributed more to the proper understanding of this writer, than to that of any of the rest. Schleiermacher, however— an accident which easily befals the love of energetic men—imperceptibly changes the Apostle into himself; makes him just as severely dialectic in his mode of thinking, just as artistic in his manner of writing; and seeing himself in Paul, rather than Paul in himself, falls into the consequence (notwithstanding all the acuteness, and the almost magical force, of his exegetical argumentation and style,—as, for example, in the Essay on Col. i. 15–20) of expounding *himself*, rather than the Apostle. Still, we cannot allow ourselves to be at all withheld by this circumstance from estimating his merit in connexion with exegetical theology so much the higher, since even in those cases in which he erred by reason of the over-might of his peculiar genius, he succeeded in awakening a larger amount of scientific life and effort in the pursuits of exegesis, than has resulted from the labours of a hundred others, who, from a want of genius and of individuality, were not even capable of going wrong.

The foundation of the University of Berlin in the year 1810, marks an important epoch in Schleiermacher's theological activity. I do not know what share he had in the proceedings connected with the actual foundation. His talented work on the Universities is said to have been not without influence in this respect. But one thing I do know,—that Berlin, just like Halle a hundred years earlier, stands for the sign of a new period in theology; and it is not an accident, but a circumstance included in that connection of things which is of higher ordination, that Schleiermacher is seen, from the very beginning, at the head of the theological faculty in the new University, as Savigny is at the head of the juristic. The spirit of the new University, in the department of theology, was indicated soon after its foundation, by the appearance of Schleiermacher's "Brief Outline of the Study of Theology, drawn up to serve as the basis of Introductory Lectures"* (1811). Only a few sheets, but a whole world of new thoughts! Theological Encyclopædia and Methodology,—as a science, a purely German necessity and production, involved in the very nature of academical studies as pursued in Germany,—had already received considerable furtherance from the labours of Nösselt, Kleucker, and Planck. But Schleiermacher leaves even the nearest of his predecessors far behind him. In his work, Theology appears for the first time as an organic whole, constructed in a wonderful manner and by a master's hand, from its practical *point of origination*,— the necessity for an orderly Guidance of the Christian Church, and the necessary interest of the theologian therein,—to its practical *summit*,—the theory and technology of the ecclesiastical praxis. Taking up, separating, connecting, arranging, with a like degree of recognition, all the essential elements of theology,—the

* Kurze Darstellung des theologischen Studiums, zum Behuf einleitender Vorlesungen entworfen.

religious and the scientific, the practical and the theoretical, the positive and the philosophical,—Schleiermacher rears with artistic genius a magnificent edifice, as well founded, as it is complete and inwardly connected. The arrangement is so simple, that every reader finds his way through it without difficulty; every theological talent and interest finds its place, its work; a vital connexion pervades the whole system; no one is permitted to be idle; only the indolent and unscientific are excluded, and that [as a matter of course, and] without the utterance of any formal ban. One does not know which to admire most in this work; the noble plan after which the whole is constructed, or the boldness and originality with which it is carried out. This ground-plan lay solely in Schleiermacher's own mind; the then existing form of theology contained merely certain first lines and essential relations, as materials towards its construction, and these, moreover, to a certain extent, were presented in a different order and connexion. Since the idea of theology from which Schleiermacher set out was superior to the then existing reality, it follows that his outline contains a theology of the future rather than of the present. In this sense it is, to a certain extent, a truly *prophetic* work, which, upon the supposition of a vital progress in our science and our church, will, as time advances, meet with increasing fulfilment. If I am required to point out what is new in the work, and what we have especially gained by it, I must call attention, first, to the intimate *connecting* of theological science with the idea of the Church, by means of which the positive, practical end, and the moral, religious interest of theology are determined; then, to the *defining* and *placing* of the notion of Philosophical Theology, at the very *portal* of the study of theology, whereby the old controversy as to the relation of theology to philosophy receives a simple adjustment; further, to the peculiar *combining* of the Exegetical, Church-Historical, and Systematic elements under the common notion of Historical Theology, by which means the injurious separation of these divisions is done away, and, in particular, in the department of Systematic Theology, the perpetually recurring intermixture of Dogmatics with the Philosophy of Religion, and of theological with philosophical Morals, is guarded against; also, to the imposing manner in which Practical Theology is constructed as an *organic whole*, and is taken up into the idea of theology as an *integrant part* of it, nay, as being indeed its crown;* and lastly, in so far as Methodology is concerned, to the thorough and decided *distinction* laid down, between that *general* amount of theological acquirement without which it is impossible for any one to be a theologian, and that *special* proficiency which is required as the condition of the properly academical form of activity.—The Outline has been objected to on account of the epigrammatic brevity by which it is characterized. But it was the very purpose of the work, that it should contain *propositions* merely; which none but masters in the science can understand without further elucidation. And although I could myself wish that the new edition of 1830 had contained a yet larger number of explanatory notes, I must

---

* I rejoice to find the work so highly estimated,—with especial reference, too, to this point,—in Dr. Nitzsch's " Observationes ad theologiam practicam felicius excolendam" (Bonnæ, 1831, 4to.). I entirely agree with him when he says: " esse (hunc librum) ante omnia a cæteris libris, quibus hoc tempore theologorum literatura vel aucta est vel inundata, plane segregandum, deinde eidem tamquam novum auctorem et antesignanum præficiendum.—E prophetico genere si veniam demum, dicat aliquis eam esse methodum, dicat quoque e poetico interiori illo vocis sensu, quo Aristoteli poetici dicuntur."

still confess that, for academical compendia, the form of brief and even enigmatical propositions, appears to me incomparably more suitable than that copiousness of detail which rather stifles than awakens the desire for explanatory lectures. In so far, Schleiermacher's Outline seems to me to be characterized by distinguished excellence with regard to its form also.

I reckoned just now as a part of what we have gained by this work, the peculiar representation which is there given of Systematic Theology (embracing Dogmatics, Morals, and Ecclesiastical Statistics) as the integrant concluding part,—the part relating to the Church's Present,—of Historical Theology in general; which latter, according to Schleiermacher's views, has Exegesis for its commencement, and Church History in the stricter sense for its middle portion. On this point, I shall meet with contradiction from some; perhaps from the majority of persons. I myself, however, am of the number of those who do not unconditionally assent to Schleiermacher's representation of Systematic Theology in the respect referred to. I am of opinion that the scientific interest from which Systematic Theology has its origin, is prevailingly of a different character from the *historical;* even supposing the *critical* interest to be reckoned along with the latter. It [the interest which gives rise to the construction of a Systematic Theology] is precisely the *systematic* interest; and specifically, not that subordinate interest which is directed towards the organic arrangement of a given historical material, but the interest which aims at a scientific exhibition of the principles of Christian faith and conduct in their absolute truth, in such a manner that all doubt and contradiction, and all inward incoherency of Christian thinking with regard to them, disappear. This is altogether a different thing from the historical interest. But, notwithstanding what has just been said, I must still abide by the assertion, that Schleiermacher, by giving this strong prominence to the positive, historical *momentum* in Systematic Theology, by pointing out the proper object and contents of the latter, in the developed dogmatical and ethical consciousness and system of teaching of the Church, and by repressing subjective caprice and individual speculation, rendered essential services, which, if not now, yet certainly hereafter, will be acknowledged with gratitude. But this leads me to speak of the work in which he has carried out the view of Systematic Theology just adverted to,—his greatest work,—that with which he closed and crowned his theological labours of a literary character among us,—his "Exhibition of the Christian Faith, according to the principles of the Evangelical Church."* (1st ed. 1821-22; 2nd ed. 1830-31).

Amidst the conflict of opinions and tendencies within the department referred to, it is a difficult thing to convince all, that with this work, a new period, a true reformation in dogmatical literature, has its beginning. I do not know anything which one could place by the side of it, in regard to historical importance, except, perhaps, in its day, the "Institutio Religionis Christianæ" of John Calvin. Even its opponents have been obliged to bear testimony, by the liveliness of their opposition and the energy of their attacks, to its stirring and searching power. A time will come, when new epoch-marking developements in Dogmatics will convert the developement of our time, involved in Schleiermacher's work, into a thing of the *past;* but, so long as there is life in our

* Darstellung des christlichen Glaubens nach den Grundsätzen der evangelischen Kirche.

science, the time will *never* come, when men shall cease to reckon the work itself as constituting one of those commanding, and as it were prophetic heights, from which new prospects of the goal, and new paths to it, are obtained and defined.

People have generally admired the dialectic skill which is apparent in Schleiermacher's Dogmatics: many, without knowing properly what it is they admire; and some, rather equivocally, with a secret dislike and a convenient fear, by which they consider themselves exonerated from the trouble and labour of studying the book thoroughly. But it is a great thing in a science, and always delightfully conducive to its progress, when a distinguished genius brings it nearer to the *idea* of strict science,—procures recognition and supremacy in it for method and order, for notional precision and strictness of connexion. Schleiermacher accomplished this service for Dogmatics in the degree in which he did, and his merits in this respect are so much the more highly commendable, by reason of the fact that his dialectic skill thoroughly overcame and practically refuted the earlier popularism and the merely outward logical method, together with the faint-hearted tendency to despair of securing a scientific form at all,—attained its object in a manner which was lively, free, and, in short, anything but scholastically dry. But this is neither the only merit, nor the greatest one, of Schleiermacher's work. Its greatest merit is to be sought in its *contents;* in this, namely,—that Schleiermacher, from first to last, gives so decided a prominence to the *positive* character of the Christian system of belief, to its most inward significance and connexion in the life of the Church. Notwithstanding all the peculiarity, acuteness, and honesty of his subjective apprehension, he has thereby contributed to give force again, in the minds of men and in science, to the objective and eternal truth of the Christian Faith, in an incomparably higher degree than others, who, in their presumed possession of purely objective, absolute notions as God himself possesses them, look down conceitedly upon the subjective Theologian-of-Feeling, (for so they esteem this skilful dialectician), as occupying a lower stage, above which they have risen long ago. Dr, Twesten remarks very justly, that "Schleiermacher, by conducting the science of Dogmatics to the facts of the Christian consciousness, as its basis and its true object, secured faith itself against the assaults of a science which mistakes its own boundaries, as well as restored to the System of Faith its own proper independence." This merit will be thankfully imputed to him even by the latest posterity; and it is quite possible, that if the intoxication of the new *absolute* science should be succeeded by a period of jejune scepticism, the Dogmatics of Schleiermacher will then become the chief armoury from which weapons will be drawn for use against the latter. We may account it a fault in this work, that the *exegetical foundation* has not, in it, the breadth and completeness which might be desired, and that the Christian consciousness is not apprehended with sufficient precision in its *original, canonical* form. But this defect is connected with an excellence which ought to be gratefully recognised; namely, that Schleiermacher regards the essential contents of the System of Faith not as a concluded *letter*, but as a free, *spiritual* stream, diffused through the entire historical life of the Church, and attaining to its complete developement thereby. At the same time, he holds fast its pure *source* in the life and teaching of the Saviour; he will not acknowledge anything which has not flowed thence; but while he is persuaded of the incessant directive and formative agency of the Spirit of Christ in the Church, illustrating Christ's word and Christ's history, he takes for granted, with a magnanimous confidence, that that which is in the Church matter of general *acceptance* and *consciousness* as having a *Christian* character, must also be precisely *the* Christian *Truth*. Dr. Twesten commends, "as one of the fairest aspects of this masterpiece, the noble tolerance which knows how to place itself as much as possible above opposing views, and without misapprehending their true character, yet to point out how the Christian consciousness may find expression in an equal degree in each of them." I do not merely *quote* these words; I thoroughly *subscribe* to them. The time is already come, in which this noble tolerance that characterizes the Dogmatics of Schleiermacher, is more and more demanded from the Protestant Church, and imposed upon it as a duty, as the true means of sustaining Christian fellowship, in opposition to the increasingly self-willed, disuniting, exclusive, and, in so far, unchristian and destructive antagonisms of the theological schools. The work, however, has, on this very account, been charged with fixing too broadly the limits within which the Christian character shall be held to apply, and with weakening down the characteristic Christian *truth*, while it widens the fellowship of Christian *love*. But the persons who bring the charge, are merely those who are not able to distinguish between tolerance and indifferentism. A man who so decidedly adheres to the characteristic contrast of the Gospel between sin and grace,—who gives so strong a prominence, and the central place in his belief, to the historical, living Christ in his absolute sinlessness and onliness, —who so unreservedly and consistently excludes the heretical deviations of Ebionitism and Docetism, of Manichæism and Pelagianism,—who so keenly apprehends and carries out the Protestant principle, without denying the elements of truth which are to be found in the Catholic,—as Schleiermacher has done in his Dogmatics,—such a man can be regarded as indifferent, only by those who are subjects of the most pitiful intolerance and bondage of the letter. If the Deistic Rationalism of the antecedent schools of theology has ever received a discomfiture, it has been in the Dogmatics of Schleiermacher. Many an assault that is now proclaimed as having led to a decisive victory over Rationalism, the latter would have overcome; the deadly wound that has been inflicted upon it by the truly *rational*, but not *rationalistic* Dogmatics of Schleiermacher, is something which it will never get over.

It is the fortune, or misfortune, of every great, distinctly individual work, to meet with manifold opposition. *Want* of understanding and *mis*understanding have, at the least, fully as much to do with this as the desire after *truth*—if not more. It has happened thus, too, in the case of Schleiermacher's Dogmatics. With the insight which he possessed into the existing state of the Church and of theology, and with his modest consciousness that the immediate result presented by him was merely *his own apprehension* of the Christian system of faith, and not the system of Dogmatics in its *absolute* form, he was prepared to be both misunderstood and assailed. His Letters respecting his " System of Faith,"* in which he endeavoured to dispose of all polemical matter, in order that it might not be in his way when preparing a second edition of the work, show how noble

* In the Studien und Kritiken for 1829, Parts 2 & 3. [These Letters are both addressed to Dr. Lücke.—Tr.]

was his manner of thinking, with regard to the attacks which he had experienced; how, namely, he looked upon every honest opponent, rather as a coadjutor in the common work, than as an opponent in the proper sense of the word. He endeavoured, in these letters, to remove the misapprehensions to which the work was liable; and, with unprejudiced readers, he has assuredly in a great measure succeeded. But even as, in the first composition of his work, he had been to a certain extent careless of possible misapprehensions, had treated many points without enough either of clearness or of precision, and was, in general, accustomed to expect of his readers (because it was his own habitual practice), that they should understand every individual detail by a reference to the whole of which it formed a part, and his Dogmatics by a reference to the connexion of his entire theological system of thought; so, too, in these letters, —partly from an artistic dread of tedious diffuseness, partly from a kind of magnanimous carelessness,—many points have been treated suggestively rather than fully, and thus a good deal of matter for misunderstanding has been allowed to remain; nay, from his manner of dealing out cuts and thrusts on the right hand and on the left, he has, perhaps, added to that which existed before. This fact has been interpreted to his prejudice, as having resulted from a feeling of haughty contempt. But the imputation is unjust. In scientific matters, he never manifested contempt towards anything, except downright stupidity, and the ill-will exhibited by persons who were of no consequence whatever. Except in such cases, he willingly entered into a consideration of the opinions of others; though it was not easy to get him to do this any *further* or any *longer* than the interest of his own mind in the cause of *truth* allowed. And so these attacks and misunderstandings will yet continue for a time; until his Dogmatics shall have succeeded in penetrating more generally into the spirit of our Church and of our theology, and in converting the truth which the work contains into a matter of common possession.

Schleiermacher was not one of those who, in the field of science, egotistically fancy that every thing begins with *them*. He cheerfully went back to the earlier stages and developements of theology, learned from them, and found in them points of connexion for his own views. This historical interest, on the one hand, furnishes an explanation of the manner in which, in his Dogmatics, he goes back to certain earlier dogmatic definitions laid down by celebrated teachers of the Greek and Latin Churches, and seeks to extract the golden grains which may be found in them. On the other hand, it has given rise to a couple of Essays in the department of Dogma-History, which are characterized by a high degree of thoroughness: one " on the Doctrine of Election," (an investigation of the Augustinian and Calvinistic theory), with which the Berlin Theological Journal for 1819 begins; the other, " On the Contrast between the Sabellian and the Athanasian Representations of the Trinity," with which the volume for 1822 is creditably brought to a close. The distinguished talent of Schleiermacher, cultivated as it had been by characteristic investigations into the history of Grecian philosophy, manifests itself in both these treatises. To the second of them, we are indebted for some new pragmatical points of view with respect to the earliest history of the doctrine of the Trinity. The former Essay looked like a work out of season, since, from its defence of the logical consistency adhered to by Augustine and Calvin with regard to the doctrine of election, it was adapted, so far as the multitude were concerned, rather to injure than to aid the Union of the two Evangelical Confessions, which had then but just begun. But when I pointed out this circumstance to him, he declared that it was his intention, precisely with a view to *serve* the interests of the Union, to excite a new discussion with regard to a matter which superficial reflection, indeed, supposed itself to have decided long ago,—but which, if the Union was to develope and perfect itself in a *scientific* point of view also, [and not to subsist merely as an *outward fact*], *must needs*, sooner or later, be brought under examination. That this difficult problem has since then been more closely and thoroughly investigated, and possibly, also, a beginning made towards new dogmatic determinations respecting it, is a circumstance for which we may thank the stirring treatise referred to.

It was not, however, merely as an *author*, that Schleiermacher laboured for the reconstruction and advancement of theology; as an *academical teacher*, also, by means of oral discourse, he opened up new paths, and furnished new points of view. When some portion of his discourses shall have been printed, it will be possible to specify more accurately the amount of gain in this direction. His lectures on the life of Jesus have given occasion to the subsequent delivery of similar courses in other Universities; and Hase's work on the life of Jesus,—an excellent book, notwithstanding all its faults,—derived its origin from the same incitement. Of Schleiermacher's lectures on the topic referred to, I know only thus much,—that distinguished as they are by the peculiar manner in which the subject is treated, they will be found to yield, when published, a measure of novelty and of stimulus, in reference both to the exposition of the Gospels, and to the dogmatical and ethical contemplation of [the person and history of] Jesus. So with regard to Practical Theology, on which he lectured regularly, and always in an enlivening, delightful manner,—Ecclesiastical Statistics, a discipline of which he was the first to establish a scientific notion at all,—Church-History, and the Historico-Critical Introduction to the New Testament, upon which he discoursed from time to time, and which he enriched with new points of view and new investigations,—and lastly, Christian Morals, upon which, mediately as an author, he exercised a reformatory influence by his " Criticism of the Doctrine of Morals" and his ethical disquisitions contained in the Memoirs of the Academy of Sciences,—all these branches of science will, as time advances, be indebted to his lectures for new tendencies and new incitements, as well amongst those who heard his discourses, as amongst those who are merely privileged to read them.

Schleiermacher was in possession of Theology as an organic whole,—not merely for the purpose of satisfying his own individual scientific necessities, or of enhancing the lustre of his genius,—but in its vital relation to the Guidance of the Christian Church; a work to which he felt himself called, both in the pulpit and in the academic chair, as an officer of the church, and a minister of the Word of God. If it is only the mutual interpenetration and vivification of the ecclesiastical and the scientific interest that constitutes the true theologian, then was Schleiermacher so much the more

completely entitled to the appellation, in that both
these elements were to be found in him, each in a distinguished degree; and withal in so beautiful an equipoise, that he was qualified to serve the Church with
equal effectiveness as a practical and as a theoretical
theologian. I have always admired and envied him for
this,—that God had given to him to be active in both
directions of the theological life with an equal degree of
eminent proficiency. His scientific activity in the study
and in the academic chair, was crowned, every Sunday,
by the preaching of the Word of God in the pulpit, and
was also variously interwoven, the whole week through,
with ecclesiastical duties in his congregation, and with
the catechetical instruction of the youthful Christians
committed to his charge. For any one else, this would
have been too much; one occupation or another would
have suffered by reason of all the rest. Not so with
Schleiermacher! I have never even heard him complain that his manifold duties were too much for him,
or that one interfered with another. On the contrary,
he seemed to find in the one refreshment and reanimation for the discharge of the other. And when I call
to mind in addition, that notwithstanding all his multiplied official occupations, and his copious activity as a
writer, he was at all times possessed of leisure, good
temper, and a lively readiness for the enjoyment of
social life in larger and in smaller circles,—that he never
brought with him into society the unwieldy gravity of the
study or the official position, but was always the cheerful,
enlivening companion,—I can free myself from the spell
of that astonished admiration with which I regard this
great man, only by considering how richly the good
God had endowed him with gifts above others, and by
delighting myself with the contemplation of his virtue

in turning them all to account, and bringing them all into a proper connexion with one another.

That which was immediately and chiefly prominent in his performance of duties connected with his spiritual office, was his Sunday's sermon; an image, and at the same time a supplement and completion, of his scientific activity. As regards the relation of his Sermons to his Dogmatics,—the manner in which the two verily agree with, supplement, and explain each other,—I may appeal to the excellent essay on that subject by Dr. Rienäcker, Preacher at the Cathedral in Halle,[*] and am certain that any one who reads it attentively will agree with him in this, that Schleiermacher, although he attached great importance to the *formal* difference between the scientific, academic lecture, and the popular mode of communication with regard to the Christian Faith, and everywhere gave effect to the distinction, yet knew so little of any *material* diversity between the two things, that one must needs say, his Dogmatics are just as indispensable to a complete scientific understanding of his Sermons, as the study of his Sermons is necessary in order to an all-sided comprehension of the former work. They are but superficial or malicious persons who, without any foundation for it, have given utterance to the suspicion that the man was a different character, in the pulpit, from what he was in the academic chair and in his scientific writings. The same fervour and love with which, in the pulpit, he held fast to the positive contents of Scripture, and made its vitally personal centre, the Redeemer, as the only-begotten Son of God, the ever-recurring theme of his sermons, appear also plainly enough in his Dogmatics, amidst the labours of the critical and dialectic understanding; and

[*] In the Studien und Kritiken for 1831, Part ii. p. 240 et seq.

the freedom and spirituality with which, in his Dogmatics, he everywhere places himself in opposition to the bondage of the letter, to the false allegoric-Gnostic, as well as to the Jewish-Christian manner of connecting the Old and New Testaments, and to the confounding of the essential and the non-essential, are prevalent also in his Sermons,—in which, after the noble style of Luther, he expected of his hearers a toleration for even the *freest* announcement of truth perceived. I have already remarked above, what a rich treasure his sermons are for the purposes of scientific exegesis, especially in relation to the New Testament. But in order that it might be fully perceived how truly Schleiermacher, in the pulpit as in the academic chair, was a man of complete, homogeneous, and symmetrical character, one of his younger disciples, Rütenick, has shown, in a very instructive manner, (in the first instance, it is true, only in a popular form,) how his whole System of Christian Morals may be constructed from the materials afforded by his sermons. Of the questionable distinction between *dogmatical* [doctrinal] and *moral* [ethical] sermons, Schleiermacher knew nothing. As, even in a scientific point of view, he admitted but a very *relative* distinction between Dogmatics and Morals, and insisted most decidedly upon the maintenance of the most intimate connexion and mutual relation between the two, so too, in his sermons, he always held fast and exhibited the most vital, reciprocal connexion as existing between Christian thought and action, between faith and love; and I do not know one of his sermons, whether printed or merely listened to, in which one would find a preponderance of the dogmatical or the ethical element, unaccompanied by a most vivid tracing out of each to its junction with the other. A complete statement of the characteristic peculiarities of Schleiermacher's mode of preaching is not my object here. The talented characteristic sketch by Dr. Sack* is a good beginning towards an apprehension, without exaggeration and without party spirit, of Schleiermacher's great merits, and his distinguished originality, in this department also. My friend designates the homiletical peculiarities of Schleiermacher as being threefold. The first, and the most fruitful of good, appears to him to be the confidence and earnest vitality with which all his contemplation sets out from a fellowship with the person of Christ by means of faith and love, makes this fellowship explanatory of the essential character and destiny of the Church, and draws from it a reliance on the power of the Spirit, which has already passed over into the Church. While he assigns to this characteristic the greatest praise, and the epoch-marking importance which belongs to Schleiermacher's mode of preaching, he finds its second characteristic, (to which he alludes rather in the way of censure), to consist in this, that the worth accorded by Schleiermacher to the Word of God in the Scriptures, is not that of ever newly *originating* his faith, and of giving to it a *Divine determination* with regard to its essential elements, but merely that of *guiding* and *regulating* his *reflection* upon his own believing feeling.† This censure, in my views, is based upon a false apprehension of the idea of faith as entertained by Schleiermacher. Dr. Sack supposes that faith, namely the faith which is peculiarly Christian, was, in Schleiermacher's estimation, *pre-*

---

* In the Studien und Kritiken for 1831, Part ii. P. 350 et seq. (in a critique upon the sermons of Schleiermacher and Albertini).

† Literally, *faith-feeling*, (Glaubensgefühl); a compound employed with an immediate reference to Schleiermacher's theory respecting the ultimate basis and essential nature of religion.—Tr.

ponderantly a feeling, unaccompanied by the consciousness of an *objective truth*. This I must deny. In his sermons, as also in his Dogmatics, Christian faith, it is true, is essentially something subjective, a subjective life in men; but its characteristic, positive, *distinct and definite character* [Bestimmtheit] to which Schleiermacher gives such decided prominence, is indeed just a product of *history*, of the life and teaching of Jesus Christ; which, as its essential contents, Christian faith receives at all times in the purest and clearest form from the Scriptures. It is true, it draws from the sacred Scriptures this its contents, not as an outward *word*, as a doctrine by nature foreign to itself, but as an entire *life*, *in* which doctrine and word have their being; and it receives the same in the Christian Church, not as something which is ever *newly* appearing and originating, but as something which by virtue of the Christian Spirit, is *present* in the community of the faithful; as something which is already known, only that it is constantly growing in vitality and completeness. Dr. Sack is further of opinion, that with the peculiarity censured by him,— which he terms, by way of reproach, Schleiermacher's *idealistic* element, but to which we should rather give, in praise, the appellation *spiritual-ecclesiastical*,—there is connected a third peculiarity manifested by Schleiermacher in his sermons, namely, that he supposes the life and operation of grace to be present in all his hearers not merely as a matter of perfect consciousness, but also in such a stage of advancement, that too little regard is had to the manifold states of defective piety and of incipient faith which nevertheless actually present themselves in our congregations; and I must certainly allow that there is such a connexion; nor can I overlook the existence of a certain one-sidedness in this respect. But on the other hand, I must declare that it has always afforded me special gratification, and has appeared to me exceedingly praiseworthy, when Schleiermacher has mounted the pulpit with this magnanimous assumption of his believing and affectionate soul, that he found the Christian congregation, as such, *already* founded and gathered together by the Lord and his Spirit, and that he was not *called* to the *first planting* of their faith, but rather to the *watering* of that which was already planted, by the unrestrained communication and efflux of his own enthusiasm and knowledge, as deriving their origin and intensity from the word of God. Schleiermacher did not overlook the different stages of knowledge and piety which exist in a congregation; he took good notice of such states as are defective. But, [in preaching], he always assumed as the starting-point, a certain *average* measure of Christian faith and life as existing in the congregation; leaving the inferior stages to another kind of instruction than that which is afforded by preaching. In an age in which there are so many who deal with Christian congregations as if the work of redemption and regeneration had not yet found a beginning in them at all, either consciously or unconsciously, or as if it had every Sunday to be commenced anew, and by this perverse fashion, weary and exasperate, rather than elevate and gladden,—Schleiermacher's opposite peculiarity is only a matter for praise.—I cheerfully subscribe, on the other hand, to what Dr. Sack says respecting " Schleiermacher's talent of combining the unity and variety of his discourse, in transparency of form, and more than logical clearness of arrangement, so as to form a whole, constructed, as it were, of but one piece." I cannot forbear copying, word for word, the whole of the beautiful passage of my friend's observations which relates to this point, even with the partial *censure* it contains,—which I, however, can allow to pass only as being rather a representation of the *well-authorised individuality* of Schleiermacher: " This precision of his thoughts," Dr Sack goes on to say, " and this clearness in their relations, combined with the noble structure and the dignity of his language, this idea-abounding and animated fulness of soul, compassed about with ecclesiastical* taste and tact, cause the fervidness of his essential tendencies to appear with a prominence which affords the highest gratification. At the same time, however, it cannot be concealed that the entire structure of the author's language is rather ecclesiastical and elevated and at the same time antique, than biblical and properly homiletical. This circumstance is connected, again, with his neglect of the Old Testament; which is the inexhaustible source for the homiletical style, so far as the more lively and the more elevated departments of the latter are concerned. One may venture to say that the author has too little of the *oriental*, in apprehension and expression,—nothing of that quality which gives to the style of Herder, (apart from its defects), so powerful a hold upon the reader, especially in his earlier writings; where he [Schleiermacher] attempts the properly rhetorical, the Bible-imitative, he is seldom happy. His strength, to be sure, lies in another department; in that of truth and gentleness, of quiet energy and constancy, —qualities which pervade his words, breathing out, as it were, from their very centre."

It is known that Schleiermacher was not in the habit of writing his sermons before delivering them. Those

---

* I should prefer to translate *ad literam*, and to say *churchly*; it would give a more exact and a more appropriate meaning; but the word is hardly English.—Tr.

which are in print are all taken from notes made while he was speaking. When I was in the habit of hearing him, there were always two of his younger friends employed in taking notes of his sermons. Any one who was aware of this, was led to admire the great gifts of the man still more. To a certain extent, the sermon did not first originate in the pulpit, inasmuch as it had been already conceived in his mind several days before, and this conception had been completely carried out, as it were, up to the moment of his delivering the discourse. But he wrote nothing down, except, (at the time of my living with him,) on the Saturday evening, the text and subject, and at the most, in addition to this, the several divisions of the latter, briefly indicated. This he called *making out his bill.** Thus, however, he entered the pulpit. Here, then, so far as its precise form, its mode of presentation, and its details were concerned, the sermon had its origin, as a living product of his previous reflection, of the animating impression produced by the spectacle of the assembled congregation, and of that mastery of his mind over the order of his thoughts and his language, which was present to him at all times in an equal degree. Any one who knew this, might observe how the artistic structure of Christian discourse arose; how, at first, speaking slowly and quietly, more in the ordinary tone of discourse, he collected and arranged his thoughts; then, again, when he had spoken for some time, and had as it were spread out and drawn together the whole net-work of thought, how his speech became more rapid, more excited, and, the nearer he approached to the admonition or encouragement which formed the conclusion, proportionably augmented in copiousness and fluency.

---

* *Seinen Zettel machen.* He seems to have been thinking of the *items* of which his memorandum consisted.—TR.

Thus did I hear him, Sunday after Sunday, for the space of several years. He was always like himself; and always attractive, by reason of his peculiar mode of treating the text, by novelty and freshness of thought, by a well-ordered method of presentation, and by fluency of speech. I have never heard of his having made a mistake in speaking, or of his having corrected himself. If one's attention was not extraordinarily enchained by the thoughts presented, one often had occasion to admire the manner in which, with his peculiar style, inclined to the construction of intricate periods, he every moment, even in the midst of the most intricate, found the right word, and never lost the clue that guided him safely to the conclusion. It is not every one that has this gift; least of all the gift of speaking before a congregation, in *all* moods and circumstances, upon *all* matters of Christian faith and life, without written preparation, and always with the same degree of fulness, clearness, and beauty. It is often the case that the *contents* suffer under the mastery, and from the extreme readiness of the *language*. This easily gives rise to a monotonous manner; accustomed trains of thought quickly return; and so of all the other vices of this kind which belong to uncalled-for extemporizing. Of all this, there was no trace to be found in Schleiermacher. He had his own manner of expression, peculiar to himself; his own peculiar circle of thought. But the affluence of his mind, and the fulness of Christian life that was in him, did not permit any of the customary vices of extemporizing to obtain in his manner of preaching; but led to the result, that the hearer merely beheld in him with complacency the highest degree of homiletical skill, and was able purely to enjoy the rich fruits it yielded. When I once asked him how he had arrived at this enviable degree of skill, he answered, that he had, very early, attained to the perception, that the highest thing to be aimed at was, not to *reproduce* the sermon in the presence of the congregation, merely by means of the memory, but to let the words arise, fresh and new, from the energy and fulness of the soul at the very moment; and that in order to become qualified for doing this, he had begun by merely omitting to write the conclusion of the sermon; and thus, proceeding backwards, step by step, (just as one leaves off by degrees a warm garment to which he has become accustomed,) he had at last attained even to that which was most difficult of all,—to refrain from writing down even the introduction.

Any one who heard but a single sermon from Schleiermacher, might entertain the apprehension that he was not intelligible, that he was not popular enough, for the more uneducated in his congregation. But upon a continued and connected hearing, this apprehension completely disappeared. He expected much of his hearers; but still, properly speaking, nothing more than familiarity with the Scriptures,—and attention. And since he knew how to enchain the latter, even in the less educated, by the freshness and spiritual liveliness of his delivery, by his constant connexion of even the profoundest Christian ideas with practical life, with the existing condition of church, family, and fatherland,—an explanation is afforded of the fact, that while his audience at church consisted indeed for the most part of the more educated class, yet people of a meaner condition, and these even from other congregations, were seen to visit his church regularly, and to listen with attention to his discourses. I believe that with the progress of time, this portion of his audience continually increased in numbers; since, just as there was in his entire theology a vital progress, so also in his mode of preaching, concurrently with the continued experience and enlargement of his inward life, there was a constant advance in the qualities of Christian simplicity and fervour, from year to year.

Preaching, certainly, constituted for Schleiermacher the principal scene of his efficiency in the congregation; but, even as he was accustomed to take a connected view of all that belonged to any particular circle of activity, so was he also mindful, and that with a like degree of love and faithfulness, of all that is included in the essential nature of the congregational life. Even before the necessity for liturgical reforms in connexion with Divine worship became more generally a matter of discussion, he endeavoured, in his own congregation, to awaken, and to satisfy this liturgical want as well as he was able to do it in his own circle, without a more general reform in the Evangelical Church as a whole. Since he regarded singing and preaching as constituting one living whole, and the hymn-book then introduced was on the contrary obstructive to the ordering of such a whole, he hit upon the expedient of getting particular hymns printed, at least for each morning service,—hymns which he selected, with a reference to their sense and suitability, from the rich treasures of sacred song, ancient and modern, belonging to our Church. Thus his congregation became acquainted by degrees with the most beautiful of our hymns, and he himself was practised and qualified for taking a leading part in the preparation of a new hymn-book, which should be adapted to our present state of Christian culture. It is known that he was one of the principal compilers of the New Berlin Hymn-Book. His defence of this collection*

* " Ueber das Berliner Gesangbuch. Ein Schreiben an Herrn Bischof

testifies to the clearness, precision, and experience of his mind in this department also.

I have no immediate information in regard to his catechetical method in the religious instruction of the young. I know only this,—that his instruction preparatory to confirmation was very much liked and sought after, especially amongst the higher orders, and that the young persons of both sexes whom he prepared and confirmed, attached themselves to him with an especial degree of cordiality and constancy. This would be inconceivable, unless, in this department of labour also, he had possessed a considerable talent for warming and spiritually animating the minds of the young in favour of the Gospel. The congregation of young persons which he thus formed for himself, was at the same time, as it appeared to me, his principal sphere for the exercise of the pastoral care. He did not withdraw himself from the discharge of this essential part of his duty as a preacher. But it was a characteristic involved in the entire nature of his position, and to some extent also in his personal individuality, that as a pastor, he rather permitted himself to be sought after by those who had affection and confidence towards him, than went himself in search of them. What he possibly sacrificed of efficiency, in this department of his spiritual office, he compensated, in a high degree, by his constant and active participation in the general concerns of the Church. Schleiermacher regarded the individual congregation as a vitally organic part of the ecclesiastical whole, inseparable from the latter both in health and in disease. His reformatory activity was directed at a very early period towards the circumstances and the

Dr. Ritschl in Stettin." (On the Berlin Hymn-Book. A Letter to Bishop Dr. Ritschl of Stettin). 1830.

necessities of the Church's life as a whole. His first publication in connexion with this subject consists of "Two Non-prejudicative Opinions in matters connected with the Interests of the Protestant Church; with a more immediate reference to the Prussian State" (1804). This document was written about the time when he had finished his profoundly thoughtful work on the Criticism of the Doctrine of Morals. It appeared without his name; but it bore the impress of his mind. In the first Opinion, which relates to the separation of the two Protestant Churches, the ecclesiastical life-question of his mind, the Union, already makes its appearance, as clearly and definitely as possible. He points out the mischiefs of the separation hitherto existing: how, in relation to the religious interest, it nourishes superstition on the one hand, and, on the other, indifference towards even the essentials of religion; then, moreover, how it also operates injuriously in relation to general morality and true culture; and again, lastly, how, in relation to the state and the school, it also shows itself as an evil which it is high time to remedy. All this is worked out in a manner distinguished as much by the truthfulness of lively experience, as by genius and wit. But Schleiermacher did not content himself with complaining of the evil; even then, along with the necessity of the Union, he also pointed out the proper manner of its *accomplishment*; he demanded that the *fellowship* of the Churches should be restored, without touching the differences in the system of *doctrine* or the variations in the *ritual*, and insisted that this restoration should be effected without circumscribing the liberty of faith and action of any individual. Even at that time, he called attention to the fact, that in the community of the United

Brethren, this idea of Union was realized in a satisfactory manner. The second Opinion inquires into the means by which the decline of religion may be prevented. Full of the most lively and truthful delineations of the corruptions, unseemlinesses, and incongruities which were to be found as well in the regulation and administration of public worship as in the constitution and condition of the clerical order, it contains at the same time a multitude of reformatory hints and proposals, which, in the revolution that has taken place in the ecclesiastical life since 1814, have in part been realized, in part agitated anew, and subjected to a fuller discussion. I do not know what impression these two Opinions made at the time of their appearance; assuredly but a very preparatory one. They contain already, however,— partly wrought out in detail, partly in the germ,—all those ideas which, ten years later, Schleiermacher began to diffuse after a more energetic and more complete fashion, and to conduct to supremacy.—It was but for a short time that he was permitted to take part in the general government of the Church in one of the higher spiritual offices connected with the State. It was at that season of the regeneration of the Prussian State, when those ministers of powerful intellect, Von Stein and Wilhelm Von Humboldt, were seeking, in every department, to place the most able men at the head of affairs, and when, accordingly, Schleiermacher also could not fail of finding his place. I do not know in what manner, nor to what extent, he exercised an influence at that period in connexion with the reform of the Church. But this I know, that he willingly withdrew from the position, when, subsequently, the troublesome quickness and decision of his mind met with more of simple resistance than of positive effect. After this he confined himself to aiding, according to his ability, partly as a writer, and partly as the freely elected President of the Berlin Synod, in promoting the conduct, upon the right basis and in the right way, of the reform of public worship and the constitution of the Church, (which had been agitated, especially since the year 1814, even in the *highest* quarter); and, along with this, of the Union. To this period belongs the series of his *occasional* publications relative to ecclesiastical affairs,—chiefly of a polemical character, and commencing with the celebrated " Letter of Congratulation to the Very Reverend the Members of the Commission appointed by his Majesty the King of Prussia for the purpose of preparing new Liturgical Forms" (1814). The anonymous guise of this work did not prevent the instant discovery of the author; so completely does it bear the impress of his mind. Rather a condolence and warning, than a congratulation, and not wanting in a certain degree of irony,—it was nevertheless received by the Commission with more than kindness. One might almost say that none of Schleiermacher's writings attained its end so immediately as this. The Commission, with noble self-denial, entered into the ideas of Schleiermacher; instead of precipitately constructing new liturgical forms, it proposed that a constitution should first be given to the Church, by means of which it should be possible to give to the needful reform, as proceeding from within outwardly, the character of a collective volition of the Church. It pertains to the imperishable renown of the King of Prussia, that he entered into this idea with all the interest of his Christian mind, and all the energy of his kingly will. It is true, the new Liturgy for the Court and Garrison Congregation at Potsdam and the Garrison Church at Berlin, was little adapted, even by the manner in which it was introduced, to give rise to the hope of a true, comprehensive reform, brought about in a proper way. Schleiermacher, like a watchman on the battlements of the Church, observant of every appearance and movement in the ecclesiastical horizon, did not omit—this time with the avowal of his name—with frankness, yet in a tone of mildness, to subject the new Liturgy to criticism, in his pamphlet "On the New Liturgy for the Court and Garrison Congregation at Potsdam" (1816); and, at the close, to direct attention anew to this point,—" that a well-ordered Synodal Constitution affords the only means of securing for the Church a legitimate co-operation towards the reform of Divine worship,—so that neither the caprice of the individual shall be able wildly to wander at pleasure in the sacred concerns of public worship, nor a fruitful and acknowledged point of union be wanting to the like-minded, who would fain enter into a mutual connexion,—nor the man of experience and of eminence be destitute of that silent, direct influence which it is proper for him to exercise.—When, then, upon the occurrence of the jubilee of the Reformation in 1817, the King, by his praiseworthy example and excellent arrangements, prepared the way for, nay, in very strictness founded, the Union of the two Protestant Churches, and, as early as the spring of 1817, the official notification with regard to the formation of Presbyteries, and the union of the Protestant clergy into District, Provincial, and National Synods, made its appearance as the result,—Schleiermacher's rejoicing over the incipient success of his fairest and most cherished desires was equalled only by the zeal with which, by counsel and by deed, with love and diligence, he sought to promote and defend the new work. His ideas, in the mean time, had found entrance and patronage in more extended circles; a number of the clergy, especially the younger part of them, had come forward as fellow-labourers and fellow-counsellors in the sacred enterprise. Schleiermacher, with thankfulness and modesty, cheerfully recognised this fact; devoid of envy, he rejoiced that he was neither the *only* labourer, nor, outwardly, the most important one. In order, however, that by the communication and discussion of his opinions and counsels with respect to certain particulars of the official notification just referred to, he might unite such as were like-minded to a deliberate and unanimous action at the Synods which were shortly to be held, he hastily stepped forth in advance, and wrote, as early as the summer of 1817, his " Observations concerning the Synodal Constitution about to be established for the Protestant Church of the State of Prussia."—When, soon after this, the Berlin Synod assembled, and as a mark of honour elected him to be its President, he fulfilled the duties of this office with such zeal, such aptness, patience, and love, that even those who had, until then, rather feared and mistrusted him, began to bestow upon him their affection and confidence; so that the labours of the Synod evidently prospered under his guidance, through the increasingly lively harmony which prevailed amongst its members. The Union, and the new Constitution of the Church, appeared at that time inseparable,—the one was the necessary auxiliary of the other. Thus, the first sign of life given by the Synod was its " Official Declaration respecting the Celebration of the Lord's Supper, to be held by the Synod on the 30th of October." Schleiermacher was the author of this document. In it, he sets forth the Union, in a brief and popular, a gentle and earnest manner, as a *purely eccle-*

siastical pacification,—*unconnected* with any settlement of *dogmatical* differences, which would be useless, nay, would lead to new divisions,—and *testified* by means of a new and common ritual in the celebration of the Lord's Supper.

Nothing could be more convincing than this simple declaration; and any one who, in the spirit of it, took part in that first united celebration of the Lord's Supper by the entire Protestant Clergy of the metropolis, will recollect how that elevating and sacred service, accompanied as it was by the animating remembrance of the as yet *undivided commencement* of the Reformation,* contributed essentially to give stability and completeness to the conviction of the verity and purity which belong precisely to this kind of union. Contradiction and misinterpretation were hardly to be looked for; at least from theologians, who must needs be acquainted with the history of the previous divisions, and attempts at union. When, therefore,—while every one at Berlin, in vigorous health, and strong generous faith, was resigning himself to the hope that the work thus commenced would go on in gladdening prosperity, Dr Ammon's† Examination of Harms's Theses‡ made its appearance,

---

* Its commencement, namely, by the publication of Luther's Theses; the special event to which the commemoration of 1817 referred.—Tr.

† The well-known *Rational Supra-naturalist*, as he has sometimes been called; author of "Die Fortbildung des Christenthums zur Weltreligion," and other works which have excited a good deal of attention. A man of great learning, both classical and modern, and a celebrated preacher; though, when I heard him about four years ago, I thought him sadly cold and dreary. Schleiermacher compared him to an *eel*, which continually slips out of the fingers of any one who attempts to catch it.—Tr.

‡ The name of Claus Harms is well known in Germany as that of a very popular and successful preacher, as well as able and fearless defender of the standard Lutheran system of doctrine. Born May 25, 1778, at Fahrstedt, a village in Ditmarsh, (the West part of Holstein), he went to

—a bitter pill for the weaklings in faith of that day,—and found fault with that as morbid which we considered healthy, and dishonoured with all manner of insidious calumnies and ignoble derision the ordinance which had been celebrated with all devoutness,—every one was roused, I know not whether more to indignation or to pity. Upon a closer consideration, however, it seemed impossible, for the sake of the cause involved, to allow the attacks of so influential and renowned a theologian upon that still recent and delicate work, the Union, to go unreproved. All looked to Schleiermacher as the natural champion of this cause; and he was not the man to let himself be long sought after, where its interests were concerned. His pen was already pointed; he dipped it in the generous indignation which Ammon's production had excited within him; and thus, in February 1818, appeared his " Letter to Mr Principal-Court-Chaplain Ammon, on his Examination of Harms's Theses." Whatever may be our judgment respecting the polemical tone of this composition, it is possible that something more of mildness and good-nature would per-

the village school until he was twelve years old; after which the clergyman of the place taught him the rudiments of Greek and Latin. He was then required to assist his father, who was a miller and farmer; and upon the death of the latter, he managed the property for his mother, until, in 1797, she disposed of it, and thus left him at liberty to follow his own strong impulse towards a more studious life. He went to school at Meldorf, and in 1799 removed to the University of Kiel, where he devoted himself to the study of theology. In 1806, the congregation at Lunden, in North Ditmarsh, elected him as their Diaconus, (Curate or Assistant Minister). Ten years later, he removed to Kiel in the capacity of Archidiaconus, becoming subsequently (1837) Church-Provost and Councillor, and (1842) *Superior* Councillor of Consistory. His numerous literary labours have all been occasioned or suggested, in a greater or less degree, by his active zeal and experience as a *preacher* and *pastor*. The "Ninety-five Theses" referred to in the text were published in 1817, as a kind of announcement of the Tercentenary Festival of the Reformation, which haps have won over his opponent, rather than vanquished him; but Schleiermacher's whole character rendered it a thing impossible for him to oppose sweet to bitter; he was fond of a *homœopathic* cure in such cases, and as Ammon had employed wit in his challenge, it was natural that Schleiermacher should serve him with wit in return, and that of a flavour both salt and bitter. I myself, however, who just at that time saw much of Schleiermacher, can bear witness, that although upon other occasions he ascribed to himself, probably in jest, a certain itching for polemics, he was actuated and guided, in the work just referred to, purely by his zeal for the *cause* at issue. If, at the same time, his strokes fell upon the *person*, this was unavoidable; because the matter seemed to turn upon his annihilating the opponent's *personal right of attack*, and making the latter *feel* that this had been done. I do not make this observation for the purpose of wounding the feelings of his antagonist, who is still living, but for the purpose of stating the historical connexion as completely as possible from my own recollections, and of defending my friend

was held that year. It would seem that the author thought to *commemorate* Luther by *imitating* him in his mode of assailing the theological and ecclesiastical abuses of his time. Harms's bold and decided assertion, in these Theses, of the doctrines of Human Depravity and Saving Faith, gave rise to a fierce and widely-extended controversy, in the course of which he felt himself constrained to attempt a more elaborate exposition and defence of the views he had put forth. See his " Briefe zur nähern Verständigung über meine Thesen" (Letters, intended to promote a better comprehension of my Theses), 1817, and " Dass es mit der Vernunftreligion nichts ist" (That Natural Religion [the Religion of Reason] amounts to nothing), 1819. The strife was maintained on both sides for a considerable time, and then dropped; its *appreciable* results, as is usual in such cases, being but small,—unless we reckon amongst them the honest, healthy celebrity which thence accrued to the author of the first challenge, and which his later years have abundantly justified and confirmed.—Tr.

against false accusations on the part of some who are ignorant of the facts; accusations which I, too, have subsequently heard.

But this was not the last conflict which our valiant combatant in the cause of the Union and Constitution of the Church had to sustain; others, incomparably more severe, were impending. No long time elapsed, before the ecclesiastical horizon was enveloped in an exceedingly ominous gloom. To the statesmen of the old school, the developement of a more liberal constitution and a more important position for the Church, was from the very first a source of great annoyance; the suspicion of a new *hierarchical* preponderance found utterance,—at first in secret, but soon, also, aloud. Mistakes, exaggerations, remissness, and precipitation, on the part of the theologians, gave a semblance of reason to the objection, that the age was neither peaceful enough nor mature enough to allow of the Church's having a constitution of greater vitality [than that to which it had been accustomed]. And as, in the department of political life, especially from the year 1819, something of crime and something of thoughtlessness, revolutionary giddiness and the fantastic tricks of a superficial liberalism, called forth a necessary reaction, and a defensive solicitude and apprehensiveness with regard to every excitement of a free and lively character seemed almost to be but a part of the duty of caution and circumspection, it could not but be that by degrees, in the ecclesiastical department also, preference should be given to the policy of stopping short and standing still, rather than to that of following up the movement which had been begun. This is not the place, nor is it possible for me, to set forth and to pass judgment upon the individual *momenta* of the reaction in ecclesiastical affairs, as they followed upon and in consequence of one another. Enough, the appearance of the new Prussian Liturgy and Agenda was the commencement and the signal of a new and in part opposite tendency, obstructive at once—at least in its immediate result—to the Union, and also to the Constitution of the Church. Schleiermacher could not, in accordance with the principles of his practical theology, approve either the contents or the form of the new liturgical arrangements. He would have been untrue to his most inward and essential nature if he had agreed to them; and it was a consequence involved in the energetic character of his mind, as well as in the nature of the position he had previously occupied, that he became the leader of the opposition. His pseudonymous publication, "On the Liturgical Right of Evangelical Sovereigns, a Theological Deliberation, by Pacificus Sincerus" (1824), struck at the root of the opposite tendency, and stirred up anew the controversy respecting the principles of law involved in the connexion between Church and State; a controversy which, in the age of indifference, had almost been laid to sleep amongst the theologians, and had merely dragged along a wretched and spiritless existence in the schools of the jurists. The consequence has been, that since that time there has also arisen in this department, amongst theologians and jurists, a more lively intercourse and conflict of diverse tendencies and opinions.—In appearance, the noble hero was vanquished. The opposite tendency has, *practically*, obtained the upper hand. But, that its supremacy is, I might say, merely *interimistic*, and that its theory, half out of fright at the consistent, logical developement of itself in the writings of Augusti and others upon this subject, and half from a consciousness of the power of truth arrayed on the other side, becomes increasingly *modified*, relaxes, and concedes, until, perhaps, a point has been found in which the true medium is situated; this is the work of the man who so long and so steadfastly maintained and led the opposition,—until so much had been conceded on the other part, that he thought he could not, without doing violence to the claims of truth and love, delay any longer at least a cessation of hostilities.* I am too little acquainted with the individual *momenta* of the proceedings with regard to the Agenda since the year 1827, in which I left my native country, to be capable of judging as to the inward motives by which Schleiermacher was influenced in his conditional acceptance of the Agenda. But this I know, that in the great concerns of the Church, he never did anything contrary to the dictates of his knowledge and his conscience, and he was just as far removed from the idle arrogance and self-will of an *absolute* opposition, as from the pitifulness of giving up a single particle of the truth, or of his convictions, for the sake of outward peace or gain. He thus failed, it is true, to reach the summit of his desires and strivings for the welfare of the Church;

* Schleiermacher's great object (see Brief Outline, § 287,) was to secure, as far as possible, the perfect combination of *freedom* with *regularity*, in public worship; to *limit* the *subjectivity* of the officiating minister, without reducing either himself or his congregation to the condition of mere *machines*. I was informed by a resident in Berlin, who is not unknown to the theological world of Germany, that Schleiermacher was accustomed *practically* to *assert* his liberty in this respect, even to the last. The Prussian Liturgy, namely, includes a general intercessory prayer, for the King, Royal Family, Army, and People of all ranks and conditions, which is usually recited after the sermon, though it *may* precede the latter. This form Schleiermacher declined to use; and substituted an *extempore* prayer, in which the same topics were taken up, and pretty much in the same order, as in the printed form. I am not aware that he attempted to vary the *other* parts of the Liturgy, to which, as being derived chiefly, I think, from certain of the ancient Liturgies, he might possibly feel less objection.—Tr.

desires and strivings which proceeded from the most honest conviction. The tragic sorrow which this circumstance occasioned, he never concealed. But, by his example, his writings, and his efficient activity, he conducted the age to a point from which, (provided the Evangelical Church of Germany does not misapprehend its true life and well-being), it will *accomplish*, under more favourable and peaceful circumstances, that of which the might of an unfavourable and tempestuous condition of the world only permitted the noble genius of Schleiermacher to make a *beginning*. No great and clear idea has ever been lost, or remained but an image of fancy and a pious wish; least of all such as, by a reference to the inmost necessities of mankind and to the nature of the case, have been so energetically made a matter of consciousness within the Church, as the ideas to which we here allude have been by Schleiermacher.

In the last years of his life, Schleiermacher saw himself involved in a controversy with two persons with whom he would rather have remained at peace. The approaching celebration of the jubilee of the Augsburg Confession furnished those two distinguished theologians, Von Cölln[*] and Schulz[†], of Breslau, with an occasion for publishing conjointly, and with a reference to certain disquieting signs of the times, a public declaration and preliminary caveat respecting theological liberty of doctrine in the Evangelical Universities, and its limitation by means of symbolical books,—in case the design should

[*] A divine of the moderate Rationalist school. He died February 17, 1833, in the forty-fifth year of his age. His principal work, a system of " Biblical Theology," was published after his death, with a memoir of the author prefixed, by his friend Schulz.—Tr.

[†] Dr. David Schulz, the accomplished editor of Griesbach's Greek Testament, and author of many important contributions to Exegetical Theology in its various branches.—Tr.

be entertained of introducing a new requirement of adherence to the Augsburg Confession.* Declaring the Augsburg Confession to be no longer adapted to represent the unity and community of faith and doctrine in the Evangelical Church, they pointed to a better future, in which, with a larger measure of agreement, and a more general diffusion of correct views, it would be possible and advisable to set up a new and more valid Confession. Schleiermacher, knowing himself to be perfectly agreed with these gentlemen in the maintenance of the Protestant liberty of doctrine against every kind of limitation, addressed a letter † to them, in which, on the one hand, he declared that there was but little ground for apprehending any new impositions of adherence to the symbolical books,—pointing out the perfectly unpractical and useless character of such impositions, and the unlikeliness, for this very reason, of their being resorted to; and, on the other hand, protested even against the *wish* that *new* confessional documents should, at any period whatsoever, take the place of the old. Looking at this letter in connexion with what Schleiermacher had written elsewhere respecting the essential character of the Protestant Symbols, (in the "Almanack of the Reformation" for the year 1819), one might possibly take offence at certain sharp points which, according to his custom, he carelessly left sticking out here and there; but the tone of calmness, pacification, and encouragement was unmistakeably prevalent throughout the whole epistle. The passage, however, which contains the greatest occasion of stumbling, is that in which, in order to show how altogether impracti-

* The title runs,—" Ueber theologische Lehrfreiheit auf den evangelischen Universitäten und deren Beschränkung durch symbolische Bücher," (Breslau, 1830).—Tr.

† In the Studien und Kritiken for 1831, Part i.

cable it is to effect the exclusion or conversion of the Rationalists by means of orthodox formularies of doctrine and liturgies, he directs attention to the fact that it is possible for many a one, perhaps, even notwithstanding the difference of his own views, to accept and to use the prescribed liturgical and other formularies,—in his own sense and meaning, namely—without our being able to say in every case, unconditionally, that this constitutes a want of truth and faith, or a *reservatio mentalis*. It was to be foreseen, that this expression,—although, in its connexion with the whole, it explained itself, as being a benevolent and excusatory, rather than a morally strict judgment with regard to a whole series of cases which are of no infrequent occurrence, especially in the liturgical praxis,—would be subject to manifold misapprehension and misinterpretation. That the "Evangelical Church-Journal" was uncharitable enough to make it a reason for charging him with hypocrisy and laxity, nay with Jesuitism, occasioned him no surprise, and as he himself says, he silently left it to the enjoyment of its gratifying discovery; but that the two gentlemen before referred to also deemed it necessary, in their double reply, to call him to account on this head, was a circumstance which caused him pain. He did not omit to answer for himself, respecting this and respecting other matters, which had been made an occasion of reproach against him, as involving a contradiction between the earlier and the later Schleiermacher; he did so in the Preface to his "Sermons relating to the Commemoration of the Delivery of the Augsburg Confession" (1831). One sees, at the same time, what pain it occasioned him to be laid under this necessity. I will not attempt to roll away all the blame of the misunderstanding from him; but his defence is sufficient to satisfy any one who knows Schleiermacher to have been just as decided an enemy of all hypocrisy and equivocation, as of the bondage of the letter. I cannot approve all that he has said with regard to the *present* significance of the Symbols, but I share with him the glad anticipation of a condition of the Church, in which the true unity and community of doctrine shall have existence and vitality in the midst of perfect liberty. In respect of the stand-point appropriate to such a discussion, however, I can but concede that he has not, with sufficient circumspection, distinguished between the two cases,—namely, that in which symbolical books and liturgical formularies are already *in* existence and *in* use, and that in which such things are *newly* set up *for* general use,—and judged them according to their difference; and the like with regard to the *momenta* of Reformation and Revolution.

It is impossible for me to speak of Schleiermacher's *theological* character and merits, without having the *entire personality* of the man, amiable and exalted as it was, brought to my recollection. I was taught to know and love his theology and his personality together; in him the one sustained and gave brightness to the other, and my experience has doubtless been the experience of several who have occupied a position of proximity to him,—that the one became intelligible and dear to a man by means of the other. If I further attempt to delineate, from the image which I retain of his personality, some of its principal features, I know well that I want the *skill* to produce a portrait such as would be worthy of him; *not*, however, either the *love* or the *truthfulness* faithfully to describe the impression which he has made upon me in an intimate acquaintance of several years' duration.

I saw him for the first time in the spring of 1816. That moment I shall never forget. I had approached him by letter some months before, and had gone to Berlin especially in consequence of the encouragement which he had afforded me, for the purpose of *habilitating* myself in connexion with the Theological Faculty there. As his letter had expressed a friendly sincerity, rather than a cordial warmth, so I found it to be with himself, too, at our first conversational meeting. It was only by degrees that the shy and timid reverence with which I had approached him, gave place to another feeling; nay, it was, at first, only increased by the admiration which the immediate presence of his powerful soul, manifesting itself in his glance and in his speech, excited within me. But just then it was least of all *my* doing, that this timidity and shyness gradually disappeared, and gave place to an increasingly cordial and confidential respect. Any one who mustered courage to *seek* him, was very soon cordially *met* by him; and then, it was not merely the cheerful and jocose kind of social intercourse by which he tempered with gentleness the oppressive might of his genius, but it was just the loving soul, opening itself, simply and naturally, to every one upon whom he had reason for bestowing his confidence. He then no longer merely permitted an approach, but came to meet the individual, in an encouraging and confiding manner, and attracted to himself all that was susceptible and in need of love towards him. I can never think of the affectionate manner in which he drew me closer and closer towards him, bestowed upon me a constantly increasing confidence, encouraged and comforted me,—without the most grateful emotion. His love was no effeminate tenderness, accompanied by ever open, caressing speech; but an earnest, compact fire, which not merely passed through the stranger mind with a magnetic softness of attraction, but also convulsed it like an electric shock,—" yet even thus, always possessed for such as abound in vital energy a refreshing charm." —Any one that did not understand and tolerate him in this guise, might easily feel himself repulsed in the midst of his approach; and thus it has happened with many, who had been accustomed to a more effeminate sort of friendship. But what he says in his Monologues is perfectly true: " I am *sure* of those who are *really* disposed to love *me*,—my interior nature; and firmly does my soul entwine itself about them, nor will it ever forsake them. They have learnt to know me; they behold my spirit; and those who once love it as it is, must love it ever more faithfully and ever more fervently, in proportion as it developes itself and fashions itself more durably in their sight. Of this possession I am as well assured as of my being; nor have I as yet lost any one that ever became dear to me in love." I am not the only one who is in a position to celebrate his fidelity and persistence in friendship. Those who occupied a still nearer position, and had been longer connected with him, will furnish a yet stronger testimony that he was one of the most faithful of men, and that he understood the noble art of *keeping* a friend, firm and warm, even in the midst of ill-tempers and incongruities.—It is a common saying, that along with a man's advance in years, his ability and inclination to form new friendships are diminished; the bloom of youth, it is said, is the proper season for laying the foundation of friendship; the later, colder, more isolating years of life are the less adapted to the purpose, inasmuch as persons of the same age become more and more rare. In this respect, too, Schleiermacher continued fresh and young; he never isolated himself. The friends of his youth were but the *stock* of the, in him never-dying, tree of friendship, which even in his latest years put forth new branches. He knew how to set aside even the disparity of years and of intellect, by the youthful freshness and serenity of his affection.

It may sound paradoxical to the ears of strangers, and of those who judge according to appearances, but I speak with perfect truth when I affirm, that over the deepest ground of his heart *love* reigned supreme, from the very first,—and, as time went on, ever more purely and more tenderly; and that even the keenness of his *intellect*, the stinging wit, the bitterness of speech with which he fought and wounded, were never able to overcome the love which was the foundation of his *heart*. I know no one that possessed so noble a tolerance, so expansive a heart, ready lovingly to judge and to bear with the most various gradations and tendencies of intellect. Notwithstanding the decision and finality which characterized his mode of thinking, he possessed a universal capability of finding out and recognizing, without envy or repining, whatever was good in others. When I lived with him in Berlin, *he* was the man who, in spite of all misapprehension, whenever he detected anything like ability, either amongst his ecclesiastical or amongst his academical associates in office, was the readiest of all to yield to it a loving recognition and eulogy. And I remember that on more than one occasion he set younger men right, when they had let fall an arrogant, intolerant judgment respecting others. " Leave me that man in honour," was his saying; " he has ability and merit, in his way."

He never had reason to be afraid of any antagonist. Nor was he ever so. He was never in want of opponents; and just as little was he in want of a mind for controversy. If he was merely attacked *personally*, so that the attack did not at the same time affect any important *cause* of which he was the representative, he never defended himself. He rebuked his adversary by his silence. For ordinary learned controversies he had not enough either of time or of egoistic irritability. But when he saw the truth, the welfare of the Church or of the State, placed in jeopardy, and thought the foe of sufficient consequence, he *never* delayed; weakly tolerance was then as far from his thoughts, as a sparing of his time and ease. Usually the first in the field, he attacked the opponent with every force, every art, and every privilege of an honourable warfare. The employment of irony, of biting wit, in controversy, he considered allowable, nay, necessary. He did not understand wherefore he should not make use of the weapons which nature had bestowed upon him, and was of opinion that when the opposite party had come forward in a spirit of self-conceit, there was nothing so effective, for the purpose of enforcing upon him the salutary feeling of his own insignificance, as the lash of a stinging wit. He had a kind of pleasure in wit, an instinctive turn that way. But amidst the enlivening use of this weapon, he strictly and diligently kept in view the cause itself which he had to defend. He practised Polemics as a *moral* duty and art to which he felt himself inwardly called by the nature of his genius and by his love to the cause. If he had once apprehended the *necessity* of a controversy, he flung himself with the whole force of his personality against that of his antagonist. The personal element in his polemical style often served merely by way of dramatic enlivenment; but it is in a far higher degree the natural expression of his hearty interest in the cause at issue, an interest by which he was penetrated in the most lively manner. His mode of controversy was not *convenient* either to himself or to his antagonist. He made earnest work of it, and drew blood. He knew beforehand that he would draw down upon himself, from this quarter and from that, evil report, hostility, anger, and revenge; he regretted this—but, for the sake of the cause involved, he willingly accepted that which, from the ordinary character of men, was inevitable. His valour was in such cases greater than his prudence. Whatever prudence he may have had, the prudence of the indolent and the cowardly was of a kind which he ever disdained.

Always, and in every age, the number of those who labour, accomplish, and produce, to the same extent as Schleiermacher, will be but small. The natural rapidity and certainty of his mental movements does a great deal in the way of explanation. What he wrote for the press had been previously so well considered and prepared, even with regard to the form, that—since he always possessed at the same time a mastery of language —he never had occasion to strike out any thing. None of his sermons, none of his lectures cost him more than the time which was requisite for a thorough meditation. A small scrap of paper sufficed for his memoranda, even in lectures such as those upon the History of Philosophy. Thus in every labour, by his various proficiency, he saved time and spirits for new intellectual acquisition and new exertion. He was, moreover, very economical with regard to time, and by this means had time for everything that his very comprehensive vocation required of him. In his latter years, certainly, I have heard him complain that he was no longer able to accomplish all that he wished. But it is precisely the most industrious and creative class of men, by whom this complaint is most emphatically made; and the *material* energy, which is also an essential requisite, does not grow with a man's years. Schleiermacher had, altogether, but a limited capital of physical strength at his command. His bodily constitution was naturally weak and delicate—at least in the years in which I lived with him —and sickly too. But what a mastery he exercised over it, compelling it, even in its sickly states, to be the servant of his mind! Labours and journeys, official activity and social life,—his body must suffice for all and obey the requirements of all. In pedestrian travelling* he always took the lead; in the evening the last to go to rest, in the morning the first to prepare for renewing the journey. I know that he has preached, and delivered lectures, when suffering from spasms of the stomach, and no one has perceived that he was ill. I have often had an opportunity of observing, that when he has been in company till late in the evening, (and it was not easy for such meetings to last *too* long for *him*), the most cheerful and animated of all who were there, —he has lectured or preached next morning, with freshness unimpaired, often as early as six o'clock. This Socratic mastery and might of the spirit over the body was a part of his inmost nature, and secured to him in

---

* It may be as well just to remind the reader, that frequently, German *professors,* as well as German students, turn the long vacation (or at least a part of it) to account in this particular way, by having recourse to the best of all possible preparations for the fatigues of a University campaign.—Tr.

age that renewed youth, with which he "smilingly saw the light of his eyes departing, and the white hair springing up between the locks of blond,"—with which, even to his latest breath, he maintained so lively a participation both in the earnest labour and in the cheerful enjoyment of life. Of the wonderful account which we have heard lately,* that "whoever has had occasion to observe him within the last three years of his life, will be able to testify that he was the subject of an often irrepressible sadness, a prostration, an inability to contend against sorrow, which was such as to excite compassion,"—of this apocryphal compassionate story I understand nothing. "A domestic calamity," it is said, "furnished the first inducement to this state of mind; or, to express myself more correctly, the death of his only son tore away the flood-gates which still dammed up the feelings of a broken existence,—broken, he himself, perhaps, knew not how.—From that time there was an affecting joy<u>ous</u>ness in Schleiermacher's preaching; the plan of his masterly discourses remained the same, but his tone, his manner, the solution of his dialectic enigmas, had undergone a change. One would not believe it, and yet he might every Sunday convince himself of the fact,—that Schleiermacher never again left the pulpit without shedding tears:" and so the story, devoid of taste or connexion, goes on still further, and becomes at last so senseless as to exhibit to us a man who shut both eye and ear, and with tears entreated his congregation to do nothing but be resigned, and "close their eyes and ears,"—and who, at last, approached with enthusiastic confidence nearer and nearer to the immediate appearance [vision?] of the Redeemer, until he was able to revel in the corporeity, the personality, in the

* Extraordinary Supplement to the Allgemeine Zeitung, No. 77, 1834.

entire actuality of the God-Man, as Thomas saw him after the Resurrection."*—What a piece of nonsense! What an unfamiliar, nay, what an *impossible* Schleiermacher has this marvellous dreamer beheld! The death of his only and hopeful son *did* communicate a most vehement *shock* to his mind. How was it possible that it should be otherwise? But a man who could so lift himself up amidst the first sorrows of his paternal heart,—go to the grave of his ardently beloved son,—and speak with such composure, such strength of faith, as Schleiermacher did,—could not, either then or afterwards, have had the feeling of a broken existence. Schleiermacher possessed by nature a very profound and powerful sensibility, but he had also an equally energetic power of mind to govern it at all times. *Long before* the death of his son, I have seen him leave the pulpit with tears in his eyes. This profoundest stirring up of his religious feeling, however, merely gave to his discoursing the full warmth of conviction; it never hindered him from thinking and speaking clearly and with power. I saw him at two different times after the death of his beloved son, but on both occasions, I found in him the same Christian σωφροσύνη with which, in previous years, he had been able to master both bodily and mental pain, and to dictate to his feeling its proper measure.

Schleiermacher has this in common with the greatest and noblest of men, that there is something animating even about his *death*. It was the reflection, nay, the glorification of his life.

* I have been at some pains in rendering the *words* of this remarkable passage; for its *meaning* I am not accountable. The reader who avoids stumbling at it on *this* account, will at least be tempted to question its *æsthetic* propriety.—Tr.

That, when the tidings of his death resounded, not merely in Berlin, but through all Germany, nay, as far as the German name extends, all was consternation and sorrow over the great, irreparable loss,—that friends and pupils, admirers, opponents, strangers, his congregation at Church and at the High School, the entire city in which he had lived, the Court, and the people, vied with one another in giving splendour to his funeral,—this is assuredly no mere outward testimony to the greatness of his name. It is much, and it is beautiful, but this is not what I have in view. I am referring to the *inward* history of his death. I have read the record of the observations, made with the attentiveness of affection, and committed to writing for the benefit of his more intimate friends, by her who in life was nearest to him, and who during his last days did not leave him for a single moment. As much of this as is suitable for a more extended circulation, I am permitted to communicate. "The temper of his mind during the whole course of his illness, was marked by a serene and gentle tranquillity, a punctual compliance with every direction; there was never a sound of complaining or discontent; he was always alike cheerful and patient, although grave, and retired within himself." "One day, when he awoke from a slumber into which he had been thrown by means of opium, he called his beloved consort to his bed-side, and said, ' I am, to be sure, properly speaking, in a state which fluctuates between consciousness and the absence of consciousness, but inwardly I am spending most delightful moments; I am constrained to be constantly in the midst of the profoundest *speculations*, which, however, are here identical with the most heartfelt *religious* experiences.' "

I find in this incident a beautiful crowning of his life

with glory. The man who had struggled his whole life long, to attain to the *higher unity of the religious and the speculative,* but who, with modesty and caution, regarded it not as the *commencement* but as the *ultimate aim* of his thinking,—*receives* it as a reward and signal of departure for the heavenly kingdom, in those moments when the outward man dies, in order that the inward man may rise, free and pure, to the perfect enjoyment of eternal life in God!

The last days and hours of his life were pervaded and irradiated by the presence of religion. Even his dreams were reflexes of his religious life and activity. " I have had such a beautiful dream," he said on one occasion, "and this dream has left with me quite a peculiar and salutary frame of mind. I was in a very large assembly,—there were many persons, familiar and unfamiliar, all looking at me, and wishing to hear from me something of a religious character; it was in the nature of an instruction, and I gave it with so much pleasure!"—Affectionately mindful of children and friends, and, in proportion as he drew nearer to the important moment, more profoundly immerged in love, as the inmost spring of his being, he said, " To the children I leave the saying of St John, ' Love one another!' " " And I charge thee," said he to his consort, " to salute all my friends, and to tell them how heartily I loved them."

He had soon become certain of his approaching death; he would have been glad to remain with those who were dear to him; he felt that he had yet much of hardness to endure, before arriving at eternal rest; but he went to meet the last conflict with composure, and with devotedness to the sacred will of the Eternal Love.

" The last morning, his suffering visibly increased, he complained of a violent sensation of burning, inwardly, and the first and last murmur forced its way from his lips,—' Alas, Lord, my pain is great!' In a deeply affecting manner he then said to his family, ' Dear children, you should now all of you go from the room, and leave me alone; I would fain spare you the woeful spectacle.'—The perfect lineaments of death presented themselves; his eye appeared to have grown dim,—his death-struggle to have been accomplished. At this moment he laid his two forefingers upon his left eye, as he often did when reflecting deeply, and began to speak: ' We have the reconciliation-death of Jesus Christ, his body and his blood.'—While thus engaged, he had raised himself up, his features began to grow animated, his voice became clear and strong, and he said with priestly solemnity, ' Are ye one with me in this faith?' to which his friends replied with a loud ' Yea!' ' Then let us celebrate the Lord's Supper! But there can be no talk of the sacristan. Quick, quick! let no one stumble at matters of form!' After that which was necessary for the purpose had been fetched, (his friends having waited with him, during the interval, in solemn silence), he began, with increasingly radiant features, and eyes in which there had returned a wonderful, indescribable brightness, nay, a sublime glow of affection, with which he looked upon those around him,—to utter a few words of prayer and of introduction to the sacred service. After this, addressing in full and aloud, to each individual, and last of all to himself, the words of the institution, he first gave the bread and the wine to the others who were present, then partook of them himself, and said, ' Upon these words of Scripture I abide; they are the foundation of my faith.' After he had pronounced the benediction, his eye first turned once more towards his consort with an expression of perfect love, and then he looked at each individual with affecting and fervent cordiality, uttering these words,—'Thus are we, and abide, in *this* love and fellowship, *one!*' He laid himself back upon the pillow. The radiance still rested upon his features. After some minutes he said, 'Now I can hold out here no longer;' and again, 'Give me another position.' He was laid upon his side; he breathed a few times; life came to a stand. The children had entered the room in the mean time, and surrounded the bed, kneeling. His eye gradually closed."

In the anguish of sorrow, and in the feeling of spiritual elevation, I have nothing to add further, save the words of Scripture, " Blessed are the dead that die in the Lord!" and, in recollection of the saying with which I once dedicated a book to him, " Be mindful of your teachers, who have spoken to you the word of God; whose end contemplate, and be followers of their faith!"

www.ingramcontent.com/pod-product-compliance
Lightning Source LLC
Chambersburg PA
CBHW061501040426
42450CB00008B/1445